The New Official

ENGLAND RUGBY MISCELLANY

England
Rugby

Note: All statistics in the book are correct to the end of the 2015 RBS 6 Nations Championship, 21 March 2015.

This edition published in 2015

Carlton Books Limited
20 Mortimer Street
London W1T 3JW

Rugby Football Union. The Red Rose and the words "England Rugby" are official registered trademarks of the Rugby Football Union and are subject to extensive trademark registration worldwide. RFU Official Licensed Product: The RFU guarantees that all profits from the sale of products and services carrying the Invest in Rugby Mark will be invested in rugby at all levels in England. Englandrugby.com/invest

A CIP catalogue record for this book is available from the British Library

ISBN: 978-1-78097-674-7

Editor: Martin Corteel
Editorial Assistant: David Ballheimer
Project Art Editor: Luke Griffin
Production: Janette Burgin

Printed and bound by CPI Group (UK) Ltd, Croydon, CRO 4YY

The New Official

ENGLAND RUGBY MISCELLANY

England
Rugby

CHRIS HAWKES

CARLTON
BOOKS

England
Rugby

CONTENTS

INTRODUCTION

The England Rugby Miscellany is the perfect volume to take to a game because it fits in your pocket, all the stories, biographies, lists and stats come in easy-to-read bite-sized chunks and, most importantly, it is all about England Rugby and the fantastic successes enjoyed by the team over the last 100-plus years.

Every chapter follows a different theme, though they do cross-reference with each other, to form a thread of history, facts and figures on almost every page. Legendary players, Grand Slams, memorable quotes, Rugby World Cups, fantasy teams, every one will get you thinking and talking. For instance, would your all Bath team have Stuart Barnes, Ollie Barkley or George Ford in the No.10 shirt? You can also learn about the famous ground-breaking heroes from the early years of England Rugby when a try was pointless – literally – but a penalty kick was gold. And, if you don't know them already, there is a section on the songs you hear at Twickenham and wherever England play, so you can learn the words, stand up, clear your throat and sing loud and proud, "Swing low, Sweet Chariot!"

Come on England Rugby fans, this book is for you to enjoy and learn. Share the passion of millions of others and support England Rugby every step of the way!

Chris Hawkes
London, Summer 2015

England
Rugby

CHAPTER 1
ENGLAND LISTS & TRIVIA

Of all the teams in world rugby, only France (with 714) have played more international matches than England's 685 (between 1871 and 2015). During that time, a staggering 1,368 players have been fortunate enough to pull on the famous white jersey. This chapter takes a closer look at the England team and at those who have played for it.

FIRST TEN VICTORIES/DEFEATS

FIRST TEN VICTORIES

1. 5 February 1872: beat Scotland by two goals to one at The Oval
2. 23 February 1874: beat Scotland by one goal to nil at The Oval
3. 15 February 1875: beat Ireland by two goals to nil at The Oval
4. 13 December 1875: beat Ireland by one goal to nil in Dublin
5. 6 March 1876: beat Scotland by one goal to nil at The Oval
6. 5 February 1877: beat Ireland by two goals to nil at The Oval
7. 11 March 1878: beat Ireland by two goals to nil at Lansdowne Road, Dublin
8. 24 March 1879: beat Ireland by three goals to nil at The Oval
9. 2 February 1880: beat Ireland by one goal to nil at Lansdowne Road, Dublin
10. 28 February 1880: beat Scotland by two goals to one in Manchester

FIRST TEN DEFEATS

1. 27 March 1871: lost to Scotland by one goal to nil in Edinburgh
2. 5 March 1877: lost to Scotland by one goal to nil in Edinburgh
3. 4 March 1882: lost to Scotland in Manchester – *the match ended 0-0, but Scotland won by dint of having scored two tries to England's none*
4. 5 February 1887: lost to Ireland by two goals to nil at Lansdowne Road, Dublin
5. 15 February 1890: lost 1-0 to Wales in Dewsbury
6. 7 March 1891: lost 9-3 to Scotland in Richmond
7. 7 January 1893: lost 12-11 to Wales in Cardiff
8. 4 March 1893: lost 8-0 to Scotland in Leeds
9. 3 February 1894: lost 7-5 to Ireland in Blackheath
10. 17 March 1894: lost 6-0 to Scotland in Edinburgh

Did You Know That?

In the game's formative years, no points were awarded; instead, matches were decided by the number of goals scored. When a team scored a try, it entitled them to take a kick at goal. In 1891, it was declared that a match should be decided by a majority of points rather than goals: a try was equal to two points, a penalty equal to three and a goal from a try was equal to five (although a side would not then get the two points for a try). Any other goal (such as a drop-goal or a goal from a mark) was worth four points. In 1893, the value of a try was raised to three points and a conversion was changed from three points to two. In 1971, the value of a try was raised once again, this time to four points. The current scoring system, in which a try is worth five points, was introduced in April 1992.

EMBLEMS

The Rugby Football Union (RFU) was formed in 1871 and accepted membership from clubs in England and also internationally. One of the first activities of the newly created union was to accept the challenge from the Scottish members to play a match against the English. The committee was charged with selecting the England team and also the team kit. It chose an all-white kit, whose jersey was embroidered with a Red Rose.

No one is certain of the reason why the red rose was chosen, but three possibilities have been offered over the years.

1. The emblem represents the one used by numerous monarchs, such as Elizabeth I.

2. It was a connection to Rugby School (where the game is said to have started); the first kit used by the school was all white, and the rose formed a part of the school's crest.

3. Two of the RFU board's members hailed from Lancashire, and they persuaded the rest of the board to use the Red Rose (their county's emblem) as homage to their own county.

Of the three possibilities, the second seems the most likely.

When a return fixture was scheduled in 1872, RFU minutes stated that both sides should wear the same uniform they had used in 1871, including the same emblems. The Red Rose, therefore, stuck, and, although it was not standardized until 1920, it has remained a part of England's jersey in various forms ever since.

ENGLAND RUGBY WORLD CUP CAPTAINS

England have appeared at all seven editions of the Rugby World Cup since the tournament's inception in 1987. During that time, five players have earned the accolade of leading their country into battle on the game's biggest stage – and this is how they fared.

1987: Mike Harrison (Wakefield)
A fleet-of-foot winger who won 15 caps for England, Wakefield's Mike Harrison was handed the task of leading a his country at the inaugural Rugby World Cup in 1987. The team was in transition – between the 1980 and 1991 Five Nations Grand Slams – and went out of the competition following a 16–3 quarter-final defeat to Wales.

1991–95: Will Carling (Harlequins)
The Harlequins centre, England's youngest captain, led the team at two Rugby World Cups. In 1991, England reached the final, where they lost 12–6 to Australia. Four years later, in South Africa, England fell to a Jonah Lomu-inspired New Zealand in the semi-finals.

1999–2003: Martin Johnson (Leicester Tigers)
The Leicester Tigers lock is one of only two men to lead England at two Rugby World Cups. In 1999, his side reached the quarter-finals (in which they lost 44–21 to South Africa). Four years later, England memorably won the tournament, and Johnson remains the only Englishman in history to lift the Webb Ellis trophy.

2007: Phil Vickery (Wasps)
A key member of England's Rugby World Cup 2003-winning pack, prop Phil Vickery led England at the 2007 tournament. He showed his leadership qualities as the team reached the final. But there was to be no repeat of 2003: England lost 15–6 to South Africa.

2011: Lewis Moody (Leicester Tigers)
Another member of England's victorious 2003 squad, flanker Lewis Moody was manager Martin Johnson's choice to lead England into battle at the Rugby World Cup 2011 in New Zealand. Under Moody, England reached the quarter-finals, but lost to France 19–12 in what turned out to be his final appearance for his country.

ENGLAND HONOURS LIST

England have been one of the most successful teams in international rugby history. They are the only team from the northern hemisphere to have won the Rugby World Cup (in 2003), and are the most successful team in Six Nations history (in all of the tournament's guises), winning the competition on 36 occasions (26 times outright). England's honours are listed below.

RUGBY WORLD CUP

Winners (1): 2003
Runners-up (2): 1991, 2007

HOME NATIONS/5 NATIONS/6 NATIONS CHAMPIONSHIP

Winners (26): 1883, 1884, 1892, 1910, 1913, 1914, 1921, 1923, 1924, 1928, 1930, 1934, 1937, 1953, 1957, 1958, 1963, 1980, 1991, 1992, 1995, 1996, 2000, 2001, 2003, 2011
Shared Winners (10): 1886, 1890, 1912, 1920, 1932, 1939, 1947, 1954, 1960, 1973
Grand Slams (12): 1913, 1914, 1921, 1923, 1924, 1928, 1957, 1980, 1991, 1992, 1995, 2003
Triple Crowns (24): 1883, 1884, 1892, 1913, 1914, 1921, 1923, 1924, 1928, 1934, 1937, 1954, 1957, 1960, 1980, 1991, 1992, 1995, 1996, 1997, 1998, 2002, 2003, 2014

Did You Know That?
England have won more tournaments (36 - 26 outright), Grand Slams (12) and Triple Crowns (24) than any other team in the Six Nations Championship (in all its guises) over the years.

Did You Know That?
The Home Nations Championship was contested 1883–1909 and 1932–1939 (with England, Ireland, Scotland and Wales); the Five Nations Championship was played 1910–1931 and 1947–1999 (with France); the Six Nations Championship (with Italy) began in 2000.

ENGLAND COACHES

In 1969, after having played international rugby for 98 years, the RFU decided the time was right to appoint a coach to take charge of the team's affairs. And so, on 20 December 1969, Don White became England's first-ever coach. Since White's appointment, the RFU has appointed 14 coaches; details of their tenures – and the team's record during that time – are listed below.

Name	Tenure	Mat	W	D	L	W%
Don White	20 Dec 1969–17 Apr 1971	11	3	1	7	27
John Elders	1972–16 Mar 1974	16	6	1	9	38
John Burgess	18 Jan 1975–31 May 1975	6	1	0	5	17
Peter Colston	3 Jan 1976–17 Mar 1979	18	6	1	11	33
Mike Davis	24 Nov 1979–6 Mar 1982	16	10	2	4	63
Dick Greenwood	15 Jan 1983–20 Apr 1985	17	4	2	11	24
Martin Green	1 Jun 1985–8 Jun 1987	14	5	0	9	36
Geoff Cooke	16 Jan 1988–19 Mar 1994	49	35	1	13	71
Jack Rowell	4 Jun 1994–12 Jul 1997	29	21	0	8	72
Clive Woodward	15 Nov 1997–2 Sep 2004	83	59	2	22	71
Andy Robinson	15 Oct 2004–29 Nov 2006	22	9	0	13	41
Brian Ashton	20 Dec 2006–1 Jun 2008	22	12	0	10	55
Rob Andrew*	1–30 Jun 2008	2	0	0	2	0
Martin Johnson	1 Jul 2008–16 Nov 2011	38	21	1	16	55
Stuart Lancaster	8 Dec 2011–present	39	24	1	13	62

Rob Andrew was appointed interim head coach during June 2008 because Martin Johnson could not take up the post for England's summer tour to New Zealand.

Did You Know That?

Clive Woodward may have been the most successful coach in terms of the number of matches England won during his tenure (59 – including the Rugby World Cup final in 2003), but he is not the most successful in terms of winning percentage (his is actually 71.08%). Jack Rowell (72.41%) and Geoff Cooke (71.43%) both have very slightly higher winning percentages.

ENGLAND PLAYERS TO APPEAR IN TV ADVERTS

It is a sign of the times and, of course, an indication as to just how high the profile of England's rugby players has become in recent times, particularly after the side won the Rugby World Cup in 2003, but you don't have to spend too long in front of a television screen these days before an England star will be flashed in front of your eyes endorsing what can be a dazzling range of products, from energy drinks to frozen fish. Here's a selection of players whose careers have taken them to the small screen.

The entire England rugby team – prior to Rugby World Cup 2011, many members of the squad could be seen in an advert for mobile phone giants O2 – England's team sponsor at the time. Lewis Moody gently waking you up; James Haskell helping you into your shirt; Jonny Wilkinson and Chris Ashton serving up your breakfast. A rugby advert at its best.

England's Jonny Wilkinson has been in huge demand following his exploits at Rugby World Cup 2003 triumph, appearing in adverts for Gillette, Adidas (alongside David Beckham), Vitality Health and Life Insurance and, most memorably, for Guinness, an ad that ends with the strapline: "Loved by the English. Adored by the French" – a reference to the tremendous success he enjoyed at his last club, Toulon, and the admiration the fans of that club had for him.

Not all adverts came born out of Rugby World Cup success, however. Pizza Hut famously saw the Underwood brothers (Tony and Rory) and their mother take revenge on New Zealand's Jonah Lomu in the months that followed the All Black winger's match-winning performance in the Rugby World Cup 1995 semi-final in South Africa.

Other adverts involving England rugby stars include:
Lawrence Dallaglio for McDonalds
Richard Hill for EasyJet
Matt Dawson for Young's Fish
Lewis Moody for Guinness

ENGLAND CAPTAINS

The following 128 players have all had the honour of being England captain. They are listed in the order they first achieved the accolade. The numbers in brackets indicate the number of Tests in which they appeared as captain and the span between their first and last Tests as captain.

F. Stokes (3 Tests, 1871–73)
A.S.G. Hamersley (1 Test, 1874)
H.A. Lawrence (2 Tests, 1875)
F. Luscombe (2 Tests, 1875–76)
E. Kewley (3 Tests, 1877–78)
M.W. Marshall (1 Test, 1878)
F.R. Adams (2 Tests, 1879)
L. Stokes (5 Tests, 1880–81)
C. Gurdon (1 Test, 1882)
A.N. Hornby (1 Test, 1882)
E.T. Gurdon (9 Tests, 1882–86)
C.J.B. Marriott (2 Tests, 1886)
A. Rotherham (3 Tests, 1887)
F.F. Bonsor (1 Test, 1889)
A.E. Stoddart (4 Tests, 1890–93)
J.L. Hickson (1 Test, 1890)
F.H.R. Alderson (5 Tests, 1891–92)
S.M.J. Woods (5 Tests, 1892–95)
R.E. Lockwood (2 Tests, 1894)
E.W. Taylor (6 Tests, 1894–97)
F. Mitchell (1 Test, 1896)
J.F. Byrne (3 Tests, 1898)
A. Rotherham (3 Tests, 1899)
R.H.B. Cattell (1 Test, 1900)
J. Daniell (6 Tests, 1900–04)
J.T. Taylor (1 Test, 1901)
W.L. Bunting (2 Tests, 1901)
H. Alexander (1 Test, 1902)
B. Oughtred (2 Tests, 1903)
P.D. Kendall (1 Test, 1903)
F.M. Stout (4 Tests, 1904–05)

V.H. Cartwright (6 Tests, 1905–06)
B.A. Hill (2 Tests, 1907)
J. Green (1 Test, 1907)
E.W. Roberts (1 Test, 1907)
T.S. Kelly (1 Test, 1908)
J.G.G. Birkett (5 Tests, 1908–11)
C.E.L. Hammond (1 Test, 1908)
L.A.N. Slocock (1 Test, 1908)
G.H.D. Lyon (1 Test, 1909)
R. Dibble (7 Tests, 1909–12)
A.D. Stoop (2 Tests, 1910)
E.R. Mobbs (1 Test, 1910)
A.L. Henniker-Gotley (1 Test, 1911)
N.A. Wodehouse (6 Tests, 1912–13)
R.W. Poulton-Palmer (4 Tests, 1914)
J.E. Greenwood (4 Tests, 1920)
W.J.A. Davies (11 Tests, 1921–23)
L.G. Brown (1 Test, 1922)
W.W. Wakefield (13 Tests, 1924–26)
L.J. Corbett (4 Tests, 1927)
R. Cove-Smith (7 Tests, 1928–29)
H.G. Periton (4 Tests, 1929–30)
J.S. Tucker (3 Tests, 1930–31)
P.D. Howard (1 Test, 1931)
C.D. Aarvold (7 Tests, 1931–33)
A.L. Novis (2 Tests, 1933)
B.C. Gadney (8 Tests, 1934–36)
D.A. Kendrew (2 Tests, 1935)
H.G.O. Owen-Smith (3 Tests, 1937)

P. Cranmer (2 Tests, 1938)
H. Toft (4 Tests, 1938–39)
J. Mycock (2 Tests, 1947)
J. Heaton (2 Tests, 1947)
E.K. Scott (3 Tests, 1948)
T.A. Kemp (1 Test, 1948)
R.H.G. Weighill (1 Test, 1948)
N.M. Hall (13 Tests, 1949–55)
I. Preece (6 Tests, 1949–50)
V.G. Roberts (1 Test, 1951)
J.M. Kendall-Carpenter (3 Tests, 1951)
R.V. Stirling (5 Tests, 1954)
P.D. Young (2 Tests, 1955)
E. Evans (13 Tests, 1956–58)
J. Butterfield (4 Tests, 1959)
R.E.G. Jeeps (13 Tests, 1960–62)
R.A.W. Sharp (5 Tests, 1963–67)
M.P. Weston (5 Tests, 1963–68)
J.G. Willcox (3 Tests, 1964)
C.R. Jacobs (2 Tests, 1964)
D.G. Perry (4 Tests, 1965)
D.P. Rogers (7 Tests, 1966–69)
P.E. Judd (5 Tests, 1967)
C.W. McFadyean (2 Tests, 1968)
J.R.H. Greenwood (1 Test, 1969)
R. Hiller (7 Tests, 1969–72)
R.B. Taylor (1 Test, 1970)
A.L. Bucknall (1 Test, 1971)
J.S. Spencer (4 Tests, 1971)
P.J. Dixon (2 Tests, 1972)
J.V. Pullin (13 Tests, 1972–75)
F.E. Cotton (3 Tests, 1975)
A. Neary (7 Tests, 1975–76
R.M. Uttley (5 Tests, 1977–79)
W.B. Beaumont (21 Tests, 1978–82)
S.J. Smith (5 Tests, 1982–83)

J.P. Scott (4 Tests, 1983–84)
P.J. Wheeler (5 Tests, 1983–84)
N.D. Melville (7 Tests, 1984–88)
P.W. Dodge (7 Tests, 1985)
R.J. Hill (3 Tests, 1987)
M.E. Harrison (7 Tests, 1987–88)
J. Orwin (3 Tests, 1988)
R.M. Harding (1 Test, 1988)
W.D.C. Carling (59 Tests, 1988–96)
C.R. Andrew (2 Tests, 1989–95)
P.R. de Glanville (8 Tests, 1996–97)
J. Leonard (2 Tests, 1996–2003)
L.B.N. Dallaglio (22 Tests, 1997–2004)
A.J. Diprose (1 Test, 1998)
M.J.S. Dawson (9 Tests, 1998–2001)
M.O. Johnson (39 Tests, 1998–2003)
K.P.P. Bracken (3 Tests, 2001)
N.A. Back (4 Tests, 2001–02)
P.J. Vickery (15 Tests, 2002–08)
J.P. Wilkinson (2 Tests, 2003–07)
D.E. West (1 Test, 2003)
J.T. Robinson (7 Tests, 2004–07)
M.E. Corry (17 Tests, 2005–07)
P.H. Sanderson (2 Tests, 2006)
M.J. Catt (3 Tests, 2007)
S.W. Borthwick (21 Tests, 2008–10)
L.W. Moody (11 Tests, 2010–11)
N.J. Easter (2 Tests, 2010–11)
M.J. Tindall (7 Tests, 2011)
C.D.C. Robshaw (36 Tests, 2012–15)
D.M. Hartley (1 Test, 2012)
T.A. Wood (2 Tests, 2013)

FASTEST TRIES

England have got off to a flying start on a number of occasions during their long history, but none of those tries have been faster than the three listed below. Here are the fastest tries in England Rugby history.

10 seconds: Leo Price
(England v Wales, Twickenham, 20 January 1923)

Flanker Leo Price scored the then fastest try in international rugby, touching down for England a mere ten seconds after their kick-off against Wales at Twickenham on 20 January 1923. England won 7–3, having repelled wave after wave of Welsh attacks – "a siege unparalleled in international rugby", according to the *Daily Mail* – before a four-point drop-goal by wing Alastair Smallwood knocked the fight out of the visitors.

17 seconds: Fred Chapman
(England v Wales, Twickenham, 15 January 1910)

It may not have stood the test of time as being the fastest-ever try by an England player, but Fred Chapman's effort against Wales at Twickenham in 1910 – the first international staged at the ground – still earns him a place in the game's record books. It remains the fastest try scored by a player on debut in international rugby history. England's captain Adrian Stoop fielded the ball from the Welsh kick-off and surprised everyone by immediately launching an attack from his own 25-yard-line that culminated in a try by Chapman in the corner 17 seconds after the start.

24 seconds: Jonathan Webb
(England v Ireland, Twickenham, 1 February 1992)

In recent times, the fastest try scored by an England player was the one scored by Jonathan Webb against Ireland at Twickenham in the 1992 Five Nations Championship. The Bath full-back got the home side off to a flying start when he crossed the line after a mere 24 seconds. It was the first of his two tries in a match that England went on to win 38–9.

England
Rugby

Did You Know That?

Scotland's John Leslie is credited with scoring international rugby's fastest-ever try. He crossed the tryline after just nine seconds of his country's match against Wales at Murrayfield on 6 February 1999, a match Scotland went on to win 33–20.

KILLED IN ACTION: FIRST WORLD WAR

These 27 England internationals died during the First World War.

Player	Date of death	Age
Harry Alexander	17 October 1915	35
Henry Berry	9 May 1915	32
Arthur James Dingle	22 August 1915	23
George Eric Burroughs Dobbs	17 June 1917	32
Leonard Haigh	6 August 1916	29
Reginald Harry Myburgh Hands	20 April 1918	29
Arthur Leyland Harrison VC	23 April 1918	32
Harold Augustus Hodges	24 March 1918	32
Rupert Edward Inglis	18 September 1916	53
Percy Dale Kendall	21 January 1915	34
John Abbott King	9 August 1916	32
Ronald Owen Lagden	3 March 1915	26
Douglas "Danny" Lambert	13 October 1915	32
Alfred Frederick Maynard	13 November 1916	22
Edgar Roberts Mobb	29 July 1917	37
William Moore Bell Nanson	4 June 1915	34
Francis Eckley Oakeley	25 November 1914	23
Robert Lawrence Pillman	9 July 1916	23
Ronald William Poulton-Palmer	5 May 1915	25
John Edward Raphael	11 June 1917	35
Reginald Oscar Schwarz MC	18 November 1918	43
Lancelot Andrew Noel Slocock	9 August 1916	29
Francis Nathaniel Tarr	18 July 1915	27
Alexander Findlater Todd	21 April 1915	41
James Henry Digby "Bungy" Watson	15 October 1914	24
Arthur James Wilson	1 July 1917	29
Charles Edward Wilson	17 September 1914	43

GOLDEN OLDIES

England have been blessed with genuine world-class players over the years, but it is those from the game's modern era who continue to attract the majority of the media's attention. Below are five players whose England careers started in the pre-First World War era whose skills would have graced an England team of any age.

ADRIAN STOOP

*Born: 27 March 1883, Kensington; **Died:** 27 November 1957, Aldershot, 74); **Club:** Harlequins; **Position:** Scrum-half/Fly-half; **Caps:** 15 (1905–12); **Points:** 6 (2 tries)*

Adrian Stoop will always be remembered as the man who singlehandedly revolutionized the way in which England played. Taking his cue from the All Blacks and the Welsh, he realized that teams posed a far greater threat if they passed the ball quickly through the backs to fleet-footed wingers. Playing at either scrum-half or fly-half, he was a crucial pivot in this new style of play, which brought him success first with his club Harlequins and then with England, for whom he won 15 caps between 1905 and 1912.

JOHN BIRKETT

*Born: 27 December 1884, Richmond; **Died:** 16 October 1967, Cuckfield, 82); **Position:** Centre; **Club:** Harlequins; **Caps:** 21 (1906–12); **Points:** 34 (10 tries, 1 drop-goal)*

Rugby was in John Birkett's blood. His father Reg had played in England's first international in 1871 and his uncle Louis had also played for England. A powerful centre, he made his England debut against Scotland in 1906, helped England to the Five Nations title in 1910, and captained his country on five occasions. When he bowed out of international rugby in 1912, he did so holding the national record for the most appearances (21) and for the most tries (10).

DANNY LAMBERT

*Born: 4 October 1883, Cranbrook; **Died:** 13 October 1915, Loos, Belgium, 32); **Club:** Harlequins; **Position:** Wing; **Caps:** 7 (1907–11); **Points:** 46 (8 tries, 8 conversions, 2 penalties)*

Danny Lambert wasn't even scheduled to play in the match that would make his name. But, called up as a late replacement for England's match against France at Richmond on 5 January 1907, he scored a remarkable five tries – still a world record for a player making his international debut. He played three times in 1908, once in 1909, and three times in 1911, again finding the French to his liking when he scored 22 points in the match (England's record stood until 1990). He was killed leading an advance at the Battle of Loos in 1915.

RONALD POULTON-PALMER

Born: *12 September 1889, Headington;* ***Died:*** *5 May 1915, Ploegsteert Wood, Belgium, 25);* ***Clubs:*** *Oxford University, Harlequins;* ***Position:*** *Centre;* ***Caps:*** *17 (1909–14);* ***Points:*** *28 (8 tries, 1 drop-goal)*
One of the earliest poster boys of English rugby, Ronald Poulton-Palmer was a centre with a tackle-evading sidestep who first made his name when he scored five tries for Oxford University against Cambridge University in the 1909 Varsity Match. He made his England debut the same year and played in every match of England's 1913 and 1914 Grand Slam campaigns. In what turned out to be his final match for England, against France at Stade Colombes on 13 April 1914, he scored four tries – a Five Nations record for England that was not equalled until 2011. His death in 1915 shocked the nation.

CYRIL LOWE

Born: *7 October 1891, Holbeach, Lincs;* ***Died:*** *6 February 1983, Surrey 91);* ***Position:*** *Wing;* ***Clubs:*** *Cambridge University, Blackheath;* ***Caps:*** *25 (1913–23);* ***Points:*** *58 (18 tries, 1 drop-goal)*
Flying winger Cyril Lowe made his name playing for Cambridge University (he was a Blue in 1911, 1912 and 1913) and was called up to play for England in 1913. He was a key member of England's 1913 and 1914 Grand Slam-winning sides, scoring a then-championship record eight tries in the latter campaign. He survived the First World War and returned to the England side in 1920, winning further Grand Slams in 1921 and 1923. When he retired from international rugby in 1923, he did so as England's record try-scorer (with 18).

LITERARY LIONS

You don't have to look too hard in a bookshop these days before stumbling across shelves packed with the life stories of England's leading rugby players. The rugby player's autobiography, a rare item in times gone by, has become commonplace – particularly after the team's triumph at Rugby World Cup 2003. Here is a selection of the best of them, listed in order of publication.

Dai for England – David Duckham (1980)
Rugby from the Front: An Autobiography – Peter Wheeler (1983)
Flying Wing: An Autobiography – Rory Underwood (1992)
The Tower and the Glory – Wade Dooley (1992)
Smelling of Roses: A Rugby Life – Stuart Barnes (1994)
Deano – Dean Richards (1995)
My Autobiography – Will Carling (1998)
Jason Leonard: Full Time – Jason Leonard (2001)
Jeremy Guscott Autobiography – Jeremy Guscott (2001)
Size Doesn't Matter: My Rugby Life – Neil Back (2002)
Behind the Scrum: The Autobiography – Kyran Bracken (2004)
Winning! The Story of England's Rise to World Cup Glory – Sir Clive
    Woodward (2005)
It's in the Blood: My Life – Lawrence Dallaglio (2008)
Dallaglio's Rugby Tales – Lawrence Dallaglio (2009)
Martin Johnson: My Autobiography – Martin Johnson (2009)
One Chance: My Life and Rugby – Josh Lewsey (2009)
Simon Shaw: The Hard Yards – My Story – Simon Shaw (2009)
Tackling Life – Jonny Wilkinson (2009)
Me and My Mouth: The Austin Healey Story – Austin Healey (2010)
Raging Bull: My Autobiography – Phil Vickery (2010)
The Autobiography: Life on the Flanks – Richard Hill (2010)
The Thoughts of Chairman Moore – Brian Moore (2010)
Will: The Autobiography of Will Greenwood – Will Greenwood (2010)
Bill Beaumont: The Autobiography – Bill Beaumont (2011)
Brian Moore: Beware of the Dog – Brian Moore (2011)
Jonny: My Autobiography – Jonny Wilkinson (2011)
*Ripley's World: The Most Enthralling Story of the Lions' Most Crucial
    Battle* – Andy Ripley (2011)

Lewis Moody: Mad Dog – An Englishman – Lewis Moody (2011)
Finding My Feet: My Autobiography – Jason Robinson (2012)
Jason Leonard: The Autobiography – Jason Leonard (2012)
Matt Dawson: Nine Lives – Matt Dawson (2012)
Bulgarian Bruises, Bloodgate and Other Stories –
  Will Greenwood (2013)
Landing on My Feet: My Story – Mike Catt (2013)
Matt Dawson's Lions Tales – Matt Dawson (2013)
What Goes on Tour Stays on Tour – Brian Moore (2014)

ENGLAND'S HOME/FIVE/SIX NATIONS RECORD

The Home Nations Championship began in the 1882–83 season
when England played Wales in front of 3,000 spectators at St.
Helens', Swansea, on 16 December 1882. England won by two goals
to nil (they also scored six tries without reply). Here is England's
record only in the Home/Five/Six Nations against France, Ireland,
Italy, Scotland and Wales.

Opponent	First year	P	W	D	L	F	A	Pts
France	1910	86	46	7	33	1273	1071	99
Ireland	1883	119	65	7	47	1443	1037	137
Italy	2000	16	16	0	0	635	197	32
Scotland	1883	118	67	13	38	1516	1088	147
Wales	1882	119	53	12	54	1428	1371	118

FIRST TO SEE YELLOW

England's 15–9 victory over France at the Stade de France on
19 February 2000 may not have been a festival of free-flowing
rugby – no tries were scored in a match in which Jonny Wilkinson
slotted five penalties for the visitors – but it was notable for one
reason. During the match, winger Austin Healey became the first
England player in history to be shown a yellow card. Lock Simon
Shaw joined Healey for a spell in the sin bin later in the match.

THE WORLD RUGBY MUSEUM

Situated in the East Stand of Twickenham Stadium and formerly
known as the Museum of Rugby (from 1996), the magnificent
World Rugby Museum was officially opened in 2007. It contains
the most extensive collection of rugby memorabilia in the world,
including more than 10,000 recorded objects, 7,000 pieces of archival
information (including books, match programmes, minutes and
club histories) and in the region of 8,000 photographs. Star items
on display include the Calcutta Cup (the trophy awarded to the
winner of England–Scotland matches), the Rugby World Cup 2003,
a photograph album relating to the British and Irish Lions' first-ever
tour to South Africa (in 1891), the original *Football Rules* produced by
Rugby School in 1845, and the Rugby Football Union's 1871 "Proposed
Laws of the Game". Permanent exhibitions include the Twickenham
Wall of Fame (which was opened by Martin Johnson, England's
Rugby World Cup-winning captain, on 3 June 2005), the Birth of
Rugby and the World of Rugby. The museum is open six days a week
(it is closed on Mondays, except bank holidays), runs specialized
seminars and workshops, and attracts more than 30,000-plus visitors
annually. Its mission statement is: "… to maintain a service of the
highest quality in order to promote the game of rugby football by
inspiring, by educating, and by entertaining visitors from all sections
of the community and all nations. The collection and associated
documentation will be preserved for use by future generations."

THE TWICKENHAM WALL OF FAME

The Twickenham Wall of Fame was installed to commemorate the
centenary of Twickenham in 2009/10 season. The first match at
Twickenham was Harlequins v Richmond in October 1909, followed
by the first international England v Wales, on 15 January 1910. Criteria
for inclusion are: a player must have appeared at Twickenham;
they must be retired; they must have achieved greatness in their
career; and they must have played a part in a memorable match at
Twickenham. The last inductees were announced in February 2010
at the England v Wales match; there are 100 players listed on blue
plaques around the stadium and also within the museum hailing from
the following countries: England (41), France (8), Scotland (8), Wales

(9), Australia (7), Ireland (8), New Zealand (7), South Africa (6), Italy (3), Argentina (2) and Romania (1).

NICKNAMES

Rugby changing rooms are, as in any other sport, a place in which nicknames are both earned and allocated, and the England changing room has been no different. Here's a selection of the best, and worst, to have emerged over the years, although you can be sure plenty of others are still waiting to reach the public domain.

36	Billy Twelvetrees
(his Irish clubmates noted that 12 x 3 (12 threes) = 36)	
Big Ben	Ben Cohen
Billy Whizz	Jason Robinson
Bumface	Will Carling
Chariots Offiah	Martin Offiah
Cooch	Gareth Chilcott
Iron Mike	Mike Teague
Johnno	Martin Johnson
Judge	Paul Rendall
Le Pit-Bull	Brian Moore
Mad Dog	Lewis Moody
Minty	Nick Easter
Mr Hollywood	Phil de Glanville
Munch	Mickey Skinner
Robolock	Danny Grewcock
Ronnie	Mark Regan
Sauce	Henry Paul
Shaggy	Will Greenwood
Shrek	Steve Thompson
Sinbad	James Simpson-Daniel
SOS	Matt Stevens
Squeaky	Rob Andrew
The Bath Barrel	Stuart Barnes
The Brand	James Haskell
The Dipper	Jeff Probyn
The Fun Bus/Flipper	Jason Leonard
The Silent Assassin	Richard Hill
Volcano	Lesley Vainikolo
Wilko	Jonny Wilkinson

HISTORY OF THE KIT

As is the case with the Red Rose emblem, there is no documentary evidence to explain why the Rugby Football Union decided the England team would wear white shirts with white shorts in their first international against Scotland in 1871. But they did and, bar the odd occasion (such as when they needed to distinguish themselves from the opposition), have done ever since. The most plausible explanation is that white jerseys were worn by most English public schools at the time – presumably because they could be boil-washed and cleaned with relative ease.

Originally, the white shirt and shorts were accompanied by the individual player's club socks (as the Barbarians do today). This practice continued until midway through the 1930 Five Nations campaign, at which point – for reasons that also remain unclear – England players started to play in dark blue socks with a white top.

The jersey remained entirely white from 1871 to 1990. But then, England's shirt manufacturers, Cotton Traders, started to sell England jerseys to the general public and, as a result, began to make regular changes to the design. In 1991, the first red touches started to appear; then, in preparation for that year's Rugby World Cup, two thin blue and two thin red hoops were added to the upper arm. The team reverted to the traditional all-white jersey for the 1992 Five Nations, but a modified jersey was introduced the following year, with a blue collar, and thin red stripes, down the outside of each arm, flanked either side by blue. For Rugby World Cup 1995, the long stripes became two hoops on the upper arm. Sponsors first appeared on the shirts in the 1996–97 season, around the same time a second kit, all blue, appeared for the first time.

Nike took over as the England team's official jersey supplier in 1997 and worked on red and white designs, creating subtle connections with the cross of St George. In 2003, England used a tight-fitting, dri-FIT jersey (designed to make tackling via the jersey more difficult) for the first time. In 2007, a new jersey featuring a sweeping red mark was introduced – and England played in a red away kit for the first time.

Canterbury produce the current England strip; it features plain white shorts and a white jersey and navy with white top socks. The alternate kit is a red shirt with navy shorts and navy with white top socks.

KILLED IN ACTION: SECOND WORLD WAR

The casualty list comprising England internationals who died in the Second World War is not as extensive as that for the First World War (14 as opposed to 27), but is, nonetheless, no less heartbreaking.

Name	Date of death	Age
Brian Henry Black	29 July 1940	33
Lewis Alfred Booth	25 June 1942	32
Paul Cooke	1 May 1940	23
Vivian Gordon Davies	23 December 1941	42
H.D. Freakes	10 March 1942	28
R.A. Gerrard	22 January 1943	30
W.G.E. Luddington	10 January 1941	46
Robert Michall Marshall	12 May 1945	27
Alexander Obolensky	29 March 1940	24
Ernest Ian Parsons	14 October 1940	34
Henry Rew	11 December 1940	34
Christopher Champain Tanner	23 May 1941	32
Derek Edmund Teden	15 October 1940	24
N.A. Wodehouse	4 July 1941	54

Did You Know That?

Prince Alexander Sergeevich Obolensky was the most well-known England international to die during the Second World War. The son of a Rurik prince, his family fled Russia following the 1917 Russian Revolution and settled in London. A winger, he won two blues while studying at Oxford University and was called up to play for England against New Zealand in 1936. He scored two tries in a memorable 13-0 victory. Known as "The Flying Prince", he won three further caps, but was killed on 29 March 1940 when his Hawker Hurricane crashed during a training exercise.

WEMBLEY AWAY DAYS

England played at the old Wembley Stadium twice. They beat Canada 26-13 in 1992, but lost as visitors, 32-31, to Wales in 1999. Wales called Wembley home when Millennium Stadium was being built, 1997-99.

TWICKENHAM

Prior to 1910, the England national rugby team had travelled around the country to play their home fixtures, contesting matches at Kennington Oval, Blackheath and Richmond in London, Leeds and Dewsbury in Yorkshire, Manchester and Leicester. But two sell-out matches at Crystal Palace in 1905 and 1906, against New Zealand and South Africa respectively, convinced the RFU of the financial worth of having their own permanent stadium.

In 1906, the RFU handed committee member William Williams and treasurer William Cail the task of finding English rugby its permanent home. They chanced upon a ten-and-a-quarter-acre site in Twickenham, southwest London – which, at the time, was literally a cabbage patch – and, after much debate, the RFU purchased the land for £5,572 12s and 6d. Construction at the site began the following year and England played their first match there on 15 January 1910, against Wales. Eighteen thousand spectators turned out to watch the game, with the best seats costing six shillings (30p). England got off to a tremendous start, winning 11–6 – their first victory over Wales since 1898.

Since then, the stadium has undergone numerous redevelopments. In 1921, a stand was built above the northern terrace. In 1927, an extension was added to both the East Stand and the South Stand. In 1932, a new West Stand was completed. Further upgrades did not take place until the 1990s, at which point new North, East and West Stands were built. A new South Stand was completed in 2006, making the stadium a complete bowl. When the work was completed, Twickenham had become the largest stadium in the world solely devoted to rugby (with a capacity of 82,000), the second largest stadium in the UK (after Wembley), the fourth largest stadium in Europe and, most importantly, the spiritual home of world rugby.

ENGLAND RECORDS AT TWICKENHAM

England have played 286 matches at Twickenham since 1910. They have won 184, lost 79 and drawn 23 – a winning percentage of 68.35. Their biggest victory at the stadium came on 17 November 2001, when they easily beat Romania 134–0. Their biggest defeat was the 42–6 loss they suffered against South Africa on 22 November 2008. Jonny Wilkinson has scored more points at Twickenham than any other player, 650, in 42 matches between 1998 and 2011.

FORTRESS TWICKENHAM

England were invincible at Twickenham between 1999 and 2004, going 22 matches unbeaten. The run began with an easy 101–10 victory over Tonga in the group stages of Rugby World Cup 1999 and included a hat-trick of wins over both the Wallabies and the Springboks, as well as a 31–28 victory over the All Blacks. The record-breaking sequence included 113 tries and a total of 1,024 points. It finally came to an end when England lost 19–13 to Ireland in March 2004 – their first defeat as reigning world champions.

MOST TWICKENHAM APPEARANCES

Pos	Matches	Player	Span
1	55	Jason Leonard	1990–2003
2	44	Martin Johnson	1993–2003
3	42	Lawrence Dallaglio	1995–2007
=	42	Jonny Wilkinson	1998–2011
5	41	Matt. Dawson	1995–2006
=	41	Rory Underwood	1984–96
7	40	Danny Grewcock	1997–2007
8	39	Phil Vickery	1998–2009
9	37	Dylan Hartley	2008–15
=	37	Richard Hill	1997–2004

Did You Know That?
By the end of the 2015 RBS 6 Nations Championship, England had played 286 games at Twickenham; a record number of matches for a country at a single ground.

AWARDS

Four former England players have been inducted into the International Rugby Hall of Fame: Bill Beaumont, Martin Johnson, Jason Leonard and Wavell Wakefield. Seven former England internationals are also members of the IRB Hall of Fame. Four of them – Johnson, Alan Rotherham, Harry Vassall and Robert Seddon – were inducted for their accomplishments as players. Two other former England players, John Kendall-Carpenter and Clive Woodward, were inducted into the IRB Hall of Fame for non-playing accomplishments. Another former England player, Alfred St George Hamersley, was inducted for achievements as both a player and a rugby administrator.

TOP 20 APPEARANCES

Pos	Matches	Player	Span
1	114	Jason Leonard	1990–2004
2	91	Jonny Wilkinson	1998–2011
3	85	Lawrence Dallaglio	1995–2007
=	85	Rory Underwood	1984–96
5	84	Martin Johnson	1993–2003
6	78	Joe Worsley	1999–2011
7	77	Matt Dawson	1995–2006
8	75	Mike Catt	1994–2007
=	75	Mike Tindall	2000–11
10	73	Steve Thompson	2002–11
=	73	Phil Vickery	1998–2009
12	72	Will Carling	1988–97
13	71	Rob Andrew	1985–97
=	71	Richard Hill	1997–2004
=	71	Lewis Moody	2001–11
=	71	Simon Shaw	1996–2011
17	69	Danny Grewcock	1997–2007
18	66	Neil Back	1994–2003
19	65	Jeremy Guscott	1989–99
20	64	Martin Corry	1997–2007
=	64	Brian Moore	1987–95

LEADING AMATEUR

The most-capped Englishman to have played exclusively as an amateur is Peter Winterbottom. The flanker made 58 Test appearances for his country between 1982 and 1993.

GOING THE DISTANCE

Simon Shaw holds the record for the longest England career. First capped against Italy at Twickenham in November 1996, the lock made his 71st and final Test appearance for England in the Rugby World Cup 2011 against France, 15 years after he made his debut.

ENGLAND'S YOUNGEST PLAYER

He may only have played ten Tests, but Colin Laird still holds the distinction of being England's youngest-ever player. The Harlequins fly-half was just 18 years and 124 days old when he was capped for the first time against Wales at Twickenham in January 1927.

ENGLAND'S OLDEST PLAYER

The oldest man to represent England is Frederick Gilbert. The full-back was 38 years and 362 days old when he made his debut against Wales at Twickenham in 1923 and, after celebrating his 39th birthday three days later, he won his second and last cap for England the following month against Ireland in Leicester.

FIRST TO REACH 50 CAPS

It is common for players to reach the 50-cap milestone nowadays, but that has not always been the case. The first man to achieve the feat was England's record try-scorer Rory Underwood. The winger made his Test debut in a 12–9 victory over Ireland at Twickenham in February 1984 and, seven years later, made his 50th appearance against Scotland (9–6) in the Rugby World Cup semi-final at Murrayfield. Underwood went on to win a total of 85 caps for England and also represented the British & Irish Lions in six Tests.

RECORD ATTENDANCES

England are one of the best-supported teams in world rugby, and whenever England play, a packed stadium is sure to follow. Below are the ten most-watched games in England's long history.

1. 82,957 – England v Australia, *Stadium Australia, Sydney, 22 November 2003*

It seems entirely appropriate that the largest crowd ever assembled to watch an England match should have been there to witness the greatest moment in England's rugby history, as Jonny Wilkinson famously drop-kicked England to Rugby World Cup 2003 glory over Australia in a nerve-wracking 20–17 victory.

2. 82,500 – Scotland v England, *Murrayfield, 17 March 1962*

It was the largest crowd England have ever played in front of in the UK, against Scotland at Murrayfield, but the 82,500 crowd saw a dour match. Both sides kicked a penalty apiece in a 3–3 draw.

3. 82,346 – England v France, *Stadium Australia, Sydney, 16 November 2003*

Jonny Wilkinson proved the hero, kicking all of England's points (five penalties and three drop-goals) as England beat France 24–7 in the Rugby World Cup 2003 semi-final.

4. 82,223 – England v New Zealand, *Twickenham, 8 November 2014*

A record Twickenham crowd were treated to a fantastic game of rugby. England's Jonny May opened the scoring for England after five minutes with a superb individual try, but New Zealand hit back, scoring three tries, and withstood a late charge from England to hang on for a 24–21 victory.

5. 82,125 – England v South Africa, *Twickenham, 15 November 2014*

A week after their narrow defeat to New Zealand, England came up just short yet again, this time against South Africa. 31–23 down after 76 minutes, Brad Barritt scored with two minutes remaining, but South Africa held on to win 31–28.

6. 82,120 – England v Scotland, *Twickenham, 13 March 2011*

A crowd of 82,120 – a record for a match at Twickenham in the RBS 6 Nations – descended on HQ for England's final home match of the 2011 campaign. And they saw a fantastic match as England ran out 22–16 winners to keep their Grand Slam hopes alive.

7. 82,107 – England v France, *Twickenham, 26 February 2011*

England maintained their 100 per cent record in the 2011 RBS 6 Nations with a 17–9 victory over France at Twickenham. Full-back Ben Foden scored the only try of the match in the 42nd minute.

8. 82,076 – England v New Zealand, *Twickenham, 5 November 2006*

England faced New Zealand at Twickenham in November 2006, seeking to end a five-match losing streak. And although they scored three tries in the match, they proved no match for the All Blacks who strolled to a comfortable 41–20 win.

8. 82,076 – England v Samoa, *Twickenham, 22 November 2014*

England finally found the winning formula against Samoa, as two tries from flying wing Jonny May and one from full-back Mike Brown helped England to a comfortable 28–9 victory – their first 2014 QBE International victory.

10. 82,049 – England v Australia, *Twickenham, 29 November 2014*

England saw out the 2014 QBE International series with a morale-boosting 26–17 victory against Australia (their pool opponents at the forthcoming Rugby World Cup 2015), thanks to a brace of tries from No.8 Ben Morgan and 16 points from the boot of fly-half George Ford.

Did You Know That?

The highest attendance at an international Rugby match is 109,874. On 15 July 2000, they crammed into Sydney's Stadium Australia to watch New Zealand beat Australia 39–35.

ENGLAND'S TOP 25 TRY-SCORERS

Pos	Tries	Player	Matches	Span
1	49	Rory Underwood	85	1984–96
2	31	Ben Cohen	57	2000–06
=	31	Will Greenwood	55	1997–2004
4	30	Jeremy Guscott	65	1989–99
5	28	Jason Robinson	51	2001–07
6	24	Dan Luger	38	1998–2003
7	22	Josh Lewsey	55	1998–2007
8	20	Mark Cueto	55	2004–11
9	19	Chris Ashton	39	2010–14
10	18	Cyril Lowe	25	1913–23
11	17	Lawrence Dallaglio	85	1995–2007
12	16	Neil Back	66	1994–2003
=	16	Matt Dawson	77	1995–2006
14	15	Austin Healey	51	1997–2003
15	14	Mike Tindall	75	2000–11
16	13	Ian Balshaw	35	2000–08
=	13	Tony Underwood	27	1992–98
18	12	Will Carling	72	1988–97
=	12	Richard Hill	71	1997–2004
20	11	Paul Sackey	22	2006–09
=	11	Manu Tuilagi	25	2011–14
22	10	John Birkett	21	1906–12
=	10	David Duckham	36	1969–76
=	10	Matt Perry	36	1997–2001
=	10	Joe Worsley	78	1999–2011

MOST TRIES IN A MATCH

Three players share the England record for the most tries in a match, five. Harlequins wing Danny Lambert was the first Englishman to achieve the feat on his international debut against France in Richmond in 1907; Rory Underwood emulated him in 1989 when he scored five against Fiji at Twickenham; and Josh Lewsey became the most recent addition to the club when he scored five times against Uruguay in a pool match at Rugby World Cup 2003.

MOST TRIES IN A SINGLE TOURNAMENT

Cyril Lowe was England's standout performer during their march to a Grand Slam in the 1914 Five Nations Championship. The winger scored eight tries during the campaign, a record for an England player in a single tournament. His haul included two hat-tricks, against Scotland at Inverleith and against France at Stade Colombes.

MOST TRIES AT THE RUGBY WORLD CUP

Rory Underwood holds the record for the most career tries at the Rugby World Cup with 11. Chris Ashton has the record for the most England tries in a single tournament – six in New Zealand in 2011.

WORLD CUP HAT-TRICK HEROES

Four England players have scored three tries or more in a single Rugby World Cup match. Wakefield wing Mike Harrison was the first man to achieve the feat, crossing the line three times in the 60–7 victory over Japan in Sydney in 1987. Josh Lewsey scored five against Uruguay in Brisbane in 2003, while Chris Ashton and Mark Cueto both scored hat-tricks against Romania in Dunedin in 2011.

RECORD-BREAKING RUN

England's longest winning sequence in Test rugby is 14 matches, a run that began with a 50–10 victory over Wales at Twickenham in March 2002. The streak included wins over the All Blacks, Wallabies and Springboks on consecutive weekends at Twickenham in November later that year and a famous 15–13 victory over New Zealand in Wellington in June 2003. It finally came to an end when England were beaten 17–16 by France in August in a Rugby World Cup warm-up match in Marseille. The run saw England amass 493 points, scoring 40 or more points in half of the matches.

Did You Know That?
Reginald Birkett is credited as being the first player to score a try for England. He did so in England's first-ever match – a 1–0 defeat to Scotland at Raeburn Place, Edinburgh, on 27 March 1871.

RUGBY WORLD CUP FINALS RECORD

OVERALL RUGBY WORLD CUP RECORD:
BY OPPOSITION TEAM

Team (Span)	Mat	W	L	D	W%	F	A	D	T	C	P	D
Argentina (1995–2011)	2	2	0	0	100.00	37	27	+10	1	1	8	2
Australia (1987–2007)	5	3	2	0	60.00	69	80	–11	3	2	15	2
Fiji (1999)	1	1	0	0	100.00	45	24	+21	4	2	7	0
France (1991–2011)	5	3	2	0	60.00	78	64	+14	5	2	13	4
Georgia (2003–11)	2	2	0	0	100.00	125	16	+109	18	13	3	0
Italy (1991–99)	3	3	0	0	100.00	130	33	+97	14	11	14	0
Japan (1987)	1	1	0	0	100.00	60	7	+53	10	7	2	0
New Zealand (1991–99)	3	0	3	0	0.00	57	93	–36	5	4	7	1
Romania (2011)	1	1	0	0	100.00	67	3	+64	10	7	1	0
Samoa (1995–2007)	3	3	0	0	100.00	123	66	+57	12	9	11	4
South Africa (1999–2007)	4	1	3	0	25.00	52	101	–49	1	1	13	2
Scotland (1991–2011)	2	2	0	0	100.00	25	18	+7	1	1	4	2
Tonga (1999–2007)	2	2	0	0	100.00	137	30	+107	17	14	6	2
Uruguay (2003)	1	1	0	0	100.00	111	13	+98	17	13	0	0
USA (1987–2007)	3	3	0	0	100.00	99	25	+74	12	9	10	0
Wales (1987–2003)	2	1	1	0	50.00	31	33	–2	1	1	7	1

RUGBY WORLD CUP RECORD BY TOURNAMENT STAGE
POOL MATCHES: OVERALL RECORD

Span	Mat	W	L	D	W%	F	A	D	T	C	P	D
1987–2011	24	20	4	0	83.33	964	341	+623	115	88	68	12

POOL MATCHES: BY OPPONENT

Team (Span)	Mat	W	L	D	W%	F	A	D	T	C	P	D
Argentina (1995–2011)	2	2	0	0	100.00	37	27	+10	1	1	8	2
Australia (1987)	1	0	1	0	0.00	6	19	–13	1	1	0	0
Georgia (2003–11)	2	2	0	0	100.00	125	16	+109	18	13	3	0
Italy (1991–99)	3	3	0	0	100.00	130	33	+97	14	11	14	0
Japan (1987)	1	1	0	0	100.00	60	7	+53	10	7	2	0
New Zealand (1991–99)	2	0	2	0	0.00	28	48	–20	1	1	6	1
Romania (2011)	1	1	0	0	100.00	67	3	+64	10	7	1	0

	Mat	W	L	D	W%	F	A	D	T	C	P	D
Samoa (1995–2007)	3	3	0	0	100.00	123	66	+57	12	9	11	4
Scotland (2011)	1	1	0	0	100.00	16	12	+4	1	1	2	1
South Africa (2003–07)	2	1	1	0	50.00	25	42	–17	1	1	4	2
Tonga (1999–2007)	2	2	0	0	100.00	137	30	+107	17	14	6	2
Uruguay (2003)	1	1	0	0	100.00	111	13	+98	17	13	0	0
USA (1987–2007)	3	3	0	0	100.00	99	25	+74	12	9	10	0

QUARTER–FINALS: OVERALL RECORD

Span	Mat	W	L	D	W%	F	A	D	T	C	P	D
1987–2011	7	4	3	0	57.14	120	138	–18	6	4	26	2

QUARTER–FINALS: BY OPPONENT

Team (Span)	Mat	W	L	D	W%	F	A	D	T	C	P	D
Australia (1995–2007)	2	2	0	0	100.00	37	32	+5	1	1	9	1
France (1991–2011)	2	1	1	0	50.00	31	29	+2	4	2	3	0
South Africa (1999)	1	0	1	0	0.00	21	44	–23	0	0	7	0
Wales (1987–2003)	2	1	1	0	50.00	31	33	–2	1	1	7	1

SEMI–FINAL: OVERALL RECORD

Span	Mat	W	L	D	W%	F	A	D	T	C	P	D
1991–2007	4	3	1	0	75.00	76	67	+9	5	3	10	5

SEMI–FINALS: BY OPPONENT

Team (Span)	Mat	W	L	D	W%	F	A	D	T	C	P	D
France (2003–07)	2	2	0	0	100.00	38	16	+22	1	0	7	4
New Zealand (1995)	1	0	1	0	0.00	29	45	–16	4	3	1	0
Scotland (1991)	1	1	0	0	100.00	9	6	+3	0	0	2	1

FINAL: OVERALL RECORD

Span	Mat	W	L	D	W%	F	A	D	T	C	P	D
1991–2007	3	1	2	0	33.33	32	44	–12	1	0	8	1

FINALS: BY OPPONENT

Team (Span)	Mat	W	L	D	W%	F	A	D	T	C	P	D
Australia (1991–2003)	2	1	1	0	50.00	26	29	–3	1	0	6	1
South Africa (2007)	1	0	1	0	0.00	6	15	–9	0	0	2	0

ENGLAND'S LIONS

The following 151 players represented both England and the British Lions in Test matches (1950-2013). This does not include the other matches played during Lions tours. These are normally against regional or state teams, or other special representative XVs.

P.J. Ackford (2 Tests, 1989)

C.R. Andrew (5 Tests, 1989–93)

A. Ashcroft (2 Tests, 1959)

N.A. Back (5 Tests, 1997–2005)

S. Bainbridge (2 Tests, 1983)

D.G.S. Baker (2 Tests, 1955)

I.R. Balshaw (3 Tests, 2001)

M.C. Bayfield (3 Tests, 1993)

W.B. Beaumont (7 Tests, 1977–80)

J. Bentley (2 Tests, 1997)

J. Butterfield (4 Tests, 1955)

J. Carleton (6 Tests, 1980–83)

W.D.C. Carling (1 Test, 1993)

M.J. Catt (1 Test, 1997)

B.B. Clarke (3 Tests, 1993)

M.J. Colclough (8 Tests, 1980–83)

D.R. Cole (3 Tests, 2013)

A.R. Corbisiero (2 Tests, 2013)

M.E. Corry (7 Tests, 2001–05)

F.E. Cotton (7 Tests, 1974–77)

M. Coulman (1 Test, 1968)

T.R. Croft (5 Tests, 2009–13)

M.J. Cueto (1 Test, 2005)

L.B.N. Dallaglio (3 Tests, 1997)

W.P.C. Davies (3 Tests, 1955)

M.J.S. Dawson (7 Tests, 1997–2005)

P. Dixon (3 Tests, 1971)

P.W. Dodge (2 Tests, 1980)

W.A. Dooley (2 Tests, 1989)

D.J. Duckham (3 Tests, 1971)

H.A. Ellis (1 Test, 2009)

O.A. Farrell (1 Test, 2013)

R.J. Flutey (1 Test, 2009)

W.J.H. Greenwood (2 Tests, 2005)

D.J. Grewcock (5 Tests, 2001–05)

J.C. Guscott (8 Tests, 1989–97)

A.S. Healey (2 Tests, 1997)

R. Higgins (1 Test, 1955)

R.A. Hill (5 Tests, 1997–2005)

J.P. Horrocks-Taylor (1 Test, 1959)

A.L. Horton (3 Tests, 1968)

P.B. Jackson (5 Tests, 1959)

R.E.G. Jeeps (13 Tests, 1955–62)

M.O. Johnson (8 Tests, 1993–2001)

B.J. Kay (2 Tests, 2005)

P.J. Larter (1 Test, 1968)

J. Leonard (5 Tests, 1993–2001)

O.J. Lewsey (3 Tests, 2005)

C. McFadyean (4 Tests, 1966)

R.W.D. Marques (2 Tests, 1959)

L.A. Mears (1 Test, 2009)

U.C.C. Monye (2 Tests, 2009)

L.W. Moody (3 Tests, 2005)

B.C. Moore (5 Tests, 1989–93)

C.D. Morris (3 Tests, 1993)

A. Neary (1 Test, 1977)

G.M.W. Parling (3 Tests, 2013)
W.M. Patterson (1 Test, 1959)
M.B. Perry (3 Tests, 2001)
I. Preece (1 Test, 1950)
J.V. Pullin (7 Tests, 1968–71)
C.W. Ralston (1 Test, 1974)
M.P. Regan (1 Test, 1997)
D. Richards (6 Tests, 1989–93)
G. Rimmer (1 Test, 1950)
A.B.W. Risman (4 Tests, 1959)
J.T. Robinson (5 Tests, 2001–05)
T.A.K. Rodber (2 Tests, 1997)
D.P. Rogers (2 Tests, 1962)
C.G. Rowntree (3 Tests, 2005)
D. Rutherford (1 Test, 1966)
K.F. Savage (4 Tests, 1968)
R.A.W. Sharp (2 Tests, 1962)
S.D. Shaw (2 Tests, 2009)
A.J. Sheridan (2 Tests, 2009)
M.A.C. Slemen (1 Test, 1980)
O.J. Smith (1 Test, 2005)
P.J. Squires (1 Test, 1977)
T.R.G. Stimpson (1 Test, 1997)

R.B. Taylor (4 Tests, 1968)
M.C. Teague (3 Tests, 1989–93)
S.G. Thompson (3 Tests, 2005)
E.M. Tuilagi (1 Test, 2013)
R. Underwood (6 Tests, 1989–93)
T. Underwood (1 Test, 1997)
R.M. Uttley (4 Tests, 1974)
P.J. Vickery (5 Tests, 2001–09)
M.W.I.W.N.A. Vunipola (3 Tests, 2013)
M.P. Weston (6 Tests, 1962–66)
P.J. Wheeler (7 Tests, 1977–80)
J.M. White (4 Tests, 2005)
J.P. Wilkinson (6 Tests, 2001–05)
J.G. Wilcox (3 Tests, 1962)
P.J. Winterbottom (7 Tests, 1983–93)
C.R. Woodward (2 Tests, 1980)
J.P.R. Worsley (1 Test, 2009)
J.R.C. Young (1 Test, 1959)
B.R. Youngs (2 Tests, 2013)
T.N. Youngs (3 Tests, 2013)

Did You Know That?

Between 1891 and 1936, 43 England players also represented a Great Britain touring side. The Great Britain and Ireland side became known as the British Lions from 1950.

Did You Know That?

England have contributed more players to Great Britain and British and Irish Lions Test teams than any other Home Nations country with 194. Wales have contributed 150 players, Ireland 110 and Scotland 79.

England
Rugby

CHAPTER 2
ENGLAND RUGBY LEGENDS

England have been blessed with a wealth of world-class players over the years – and choosing the very best of them is no easy task and one, no doubt, that will provoke endless debate among rugby fans. However, the following ten players would appear high on any list of all-time England rugby greats.

BILL BEAUMONT

A formidable lineout jumper and an iron man in mauls, Bill Beaumont rose to prominence with some standout performances for Lancashire club Fylde, and made his debut for England in 1975, aged 22, as a replacement for the injured Roger Uttley against Ireland in Dublin. He had to wait until that summer's tour to Australia before finally nailing down a place in the starting XV, but once he had, he did not look back. He was probably unlucky not be be in the initial British Lions tour to New Zealand in 1977, but called up as a replacement for compatriot Nigel Horton. He ignored the advice of Willie Duggan, who suggested he should go straight back home, to graft his way into the Test team. The Lions may have suffered a 3–1 series defeat, but Beaumont was one of the few to return home with his reputation enhanced.

When, in 1978, England looked for a new leader to arrest their stuttering fortunes (they had won only two Five Nations matches in two years), they turned to Beaumont. His impact was far from immediate, as England won only twice in the 1978 Five Nations (against Scotland at Murrayfield and at home to Ireland) and once in 1979 (at home to France), but it all came together in 1980 as England swept all before them to record their first Grand Slam since 1957. As Beaumont left the field following England's 30–18 Grand Slam-securing victory over Scotland at Murrayfield (at the same time, they also won the Triple Crown and Calcutta Cup), he must have done so knowing his place among the pantheon of his country's all-time greats was secure.

Later that year he led the British Lions on their tour to South Africa, becoming the first Englishman to lead the Lions since Douglas Prentice in 1930. And although the Beaumont-led Lions pack dominated the Springbok pack, the tourists suffered from a lack of incision among their three-quarters and suffered a 3–1 series defeat.

For England, there would be no repeat of the glories of 1980. England won just twice in the 1981 Five Nations and, as injuries started to catch up with him, Beaumont won the last of his 34 caps (21 of which had come as captain), during the 9–9 draw against Scotland in the opening match of the 1982 Five Nations.

He was involved with the Lions once again in 2005, serving as team manager during the disastrous 2005 tour to New Zealand, and served as vice-president on the IRB Council between 2007 and 2008. He was awarded an OBE for services to rugby in the Queen's birthday honours' list in 2008 and was elected as chairman of the RFU in 2012.

FOR THE RECORD

Born	9 March 1952, Preston
Club	Fylde (1969–82)
England caps	34
Matches as captain	21
England points	0
British Lions Tests	7
British Lions points	0
RWC appearances	0
RWC points	0
Debut	v Ireland at Lansdowne Road on 18 January 1975
Last match	v Scotland at Murrayfield on 16 January 1982

HONOURS

5 Nations titles	1 – 1980
Triple Crowns	1 – 1980
Grand Slams	1 – 1980
RWC appearances	0
RWC honours	0

Did You Know That?

Bill Beaumont went on to find further fame as a team captain on the BBC's popular quiz show A Question of Sport. *He remains the longest-serving team captain in the programme's history (1981–96) and is the only team captain to have also presented the show – standing in for regular presenter David Coleman twice in 1989.*

WILL CARLING

New England coach Geoff Cooke was charged with leading England into a bright new era following the team's quarter-final defeat to Wales in Rugby World Cup 1987. After two wins in four matches in the 1988 Five Nations Championship, he turned to Will Carling. In doing so, the Harlequins centre became the youngest England captain in history. To many it was an eyebrow-raising choice: by that stage, Carling had a mere six caps to his name – and there were many more senior players in the side who might well have expected the role. But it would prove to be an inspirational selection.

The bright new era got off to an electrifying start when England recorded a surprise 28–19 victory over Australia at Twickenham. They then finished second in both the 1989 and 1990 Five Nations Championship (losing out to Scotland in a tense, winner-takes-all Grand-Slam decider at Murrayfield in the latter). The rewards might not have come their way, but England under Carling were starting to win the public's affection. They romped to a first Grand Slam in 11 years in 1991; it was perfect preparation for the Rugby World Cup (on home soil) later in the year.

And how close they came: wins over France in Paris (19–10) and Scotland at Murrayfield (9–6) set up a final against Australia at Twickenham. England fell just short, losing the match 12–6.

The Rugby World Cup pain was eased when England cantered to a second-successive Grand Slam in 1992 (their first back-to-back Slams for 68 years), and although England could not repeat their successes in either 1993 or 1994 (finishing fourth in the former and second in the latter), a third Grand Slam in five years in 1995 saw them head to that year's Rugby World Cup in South Africa with genuine hope of going one stage further than they had done in 1991. But despite a morale-boosting 25–22 quarter-final victory over defending champions Australia, England dreams were ended by a Jonah Lomu-inspired New Zealand in the semi-final at Cape Town. New Zealand won 49–25, as England conceded 25 points in as many first-half minutes. Although they "won" the second half 26–24 the damage was done). Carling was moved to describe four-try Lomu as a "freak".

England Rugby

For many, a second Rugby World Cup disappointment might have signalled the end of the road, but not Carling. Although he resigned the captaincy (following a record 58 appearances as captain) at the end of the 1996 Five Nations, he continued to be selected for the team, often at the expense of his former centre partner Jeremy Guscott. Carling made the last of his 72 England appearances against Wales in Cardiff on 15 March 1997.

FOR THE RECORD

Born	12 December 1965, Bradford-on-Avon
Club	Harlequins (1987–2000)
England caps	72
Matches as captain	58
England points	54 (12 tries)
British Lions Tests	1
British Lions points	0
RWC appearances	11 – 1991, 1995
RWC points	18 (4 tries)
Debut	v France, Paris, 16 January 1988
Last match	v Wales, Cardiff, 15 March 1997

HONOURS

Five Nations titles	4 – 1991, 1992, 1995, 1996
Triple Crowns	4 – 1991, 1992, 1995, 1996
Grand Slams	3 – 1991, 1992, 1995
RWC honours	Runner-up – 1991
	Semi-finalist – 1995

Did You Know That?
Not only was Will Carling England's youngest-ever and longest-serving captain, he was also his country's most successful one in terms of matches won. England won 44 matches during Carling's eight-year stint as captain.

LAWRENCE DALLAGLIO

Aggressive with ball in hand (he always seemed to cross the gain-line) and granite-like in defence, Ampleforth-educated Lawrence Dallaglio first came to prominence when he played a leading role in England's surprise victory at the 1993 Sevens Rugby World Cup. The Wasps man made his international debut during England's 24–14 defeat to South Africa at Twickenham in November 1995 and soon cemented a regular place for himself in England's back row. He played in all three Tests for the British Lions in their 2–1 series victory over South Africa (in what would be the only Lions Test appearances of his career), and when he was handed the England captaincy by Clive Woodward in the autumn of 1997, he was the undoubted golden boy of English rugby.

He led England to the Triple Crown in the 1998 Five Nations (England finished second behind Grand Slam-winning France), but had to stand aside because of newspaper allegations which could not be substantiated. However, Dallaglio was able to return to the England ranks (under new captain Martin Johnson) in time for Rugby World Cup 1999.

The period from 2000 onwards best defined his career. Alongside Richard Hill and Neil Back, the trio went on to form one of the most feared back rows in rugby history, and provided the heartbeat to what would become the most successful England side in history, culminating, of course, with that memorable Rugby World Cup final victory against Australia in 2003 – tellingly, Dallaglio was the only member of the England squad to play every minute of every game during the tournament.

Others left the scene following English rugby's greatest moment, but Dallaglio carried on, assuming the captaincy for the second time in the wake of Martin Johnson's retirement, and leading England through what turned out to be a disappointing 2004 RBS 6 Nations Championship (during which England lost to both Ireland and France). He retired from England duty at the end of the tournament, but after gaining selection for the British Lions tour to New Zealand in 2005 (during which he suffered a serious knee injury), he had a change of heart and returned to the international fold in 2006. He played a part in England's ride to the Rugby World Cup 2007 final, after which he retired for good with 85 caps to his name and his place among the all-time England greats truly cemented. His total of 17 tries is the most for any England forward, one more than his long-time back-row team-mate Neil Back.

Dallaglio continued to play with distinction for Wasps until the end of the 2008 season, since when he has forged a new career as a television pundit.

FOR THE RECORD

Born	10 August 1972, Shepherd's Bush, London
Club	Wasps (1990–2008)
England caps	85
Matches as captain	22
England points	85 (17 tries)
British Lions Tests	3
British Lions points	0
RWC appearances	17
RWC points	5 (1 try)
Debut	v South Africa, Twickenham, 18 November 1995
Last match	v South Africa, St Denis, 20 October 2007

HONOURS

Five/Six Nations titles	4 – 1996, 2000, 2001, 2003
Triple Crowns	5 – 1996, 1997, 1998, 2002, 2003
Grand Slams	1 – 2003
RWC honours	Winner – 2003
	Runner-up – 2007
	Quarter-finalist – 1999

Did You Know That?
As a 13-year-old in the King's House School choir, Dallaglio and 20 other choristers sang backing vocals on Tina Turner's hit song "We Don't Need Another Hero".

DAVID DUCKHAM

Elusive and creative with a blistering turn of pace, a devastating side-step (which to this day remains one of the most famous in international rugby history) and an aggressive hand-off, Coventry's David Duckham ranks as one of the most talented players ever to pull on an England shirt. He made his international debut for England at centre (alongside John Spencer) against Ireland at Lansdowne Road in the 1969 Five Nations, and although England went on to lose the match 17–15, Duckham showed his talent by scoring an eye-catching solo try from 60 yards out. In December that year, he was part of the England side that beat South Africa 11–9 at Twickenham – England's first-ever victory against the Springboks.

From 1971 onwards he generally played on the wing – and it was in this position that he forged his reputation as one of the world's best players, even though the England side in which he played struggled. Not once during Duckham's time with England did they win more than two Five Nations game in a season. "There was not one of us who felt that his place was secure," Duckham would later say. "The side was never settled, and morale was pitifully low."

Perhaps it came as no surprise then that some of Duckham's most memorable performances came with the British Lions. In 1971, relishing the opportunity handed to him by coach Carwyn Jones to play a more expansive game, and flourishing in the company of the British Isles' best players, he played a leading role in the Lions' 2–1 series victory over New Zealand, featuring in three of the four Tests, and scoring an impressive 11 tries in 16 appearances – his six-try haul for the midweek side against West Coast/Buller remains an all-time Lions record (shared with Wales wing J.J. Williams).

He was one of only three Englishmen (alongside John Pullin and Bob Wilkinson) to play for the Barbarians in the much-feted 23–11 victory over New Zealand at Cardiff Arms Park in 1973, and he played his part in Gareth Edwards' try, dubbed by many to be the greatest try of all time. So impressed were the Welsh with his performance that day, they gave him the nickname "Dai", simply because he played the game like one of them.

Duckham made the last of his 36 England appearances against Scotland in the final round of matches in the 1976 Five Nations at Murrayfield. By the time he retired, he was one of only three

Englishmen – with Cyril Lowe (18) and John Birkett (10) – to have scored ten tries or more in international rugby. He was awarded an OBE for services to rugby in 1977, continued playing for hometown club Coventry until 1979, and has since gone on to become Honorary President of the rugby charity Wooden Spoon.

FOR THE RECORD

Born	28 January 1946, Coventry
Club	Coventry (1967–79)
England caps	36
Matches as captain	0
England points	36 (10 tries)
British Lions Tests	3
British Lions points	0
RWC appearances	0
RWC points	0
Debut	v Ireland, Dublin, 8 February 1969
Last game	v Scotland, Edinburgh, 21 February 1976

HONOURS

Five Nations titles	0
Triple Crowns	0
Grand Slams	0
RWC honours	None

Did You Know That?
For a player of such undoubted attacking prowess, David Duckham had a surprisingly low try-scoring record for England (10 tries in 39 matches). He scored two tries in an international match only twice – against Scotland at Twickenham on 15 March 1969 and against France at Twickenham on 24 February 1973 – and once went 15 matches (over a period of three years) without scoring for his country. It was unfortunate for one of England's finest-ever attacking talents that he played in an era when his surrounding cast could not provide him with the chances to show his true class.

JEREMY GUSCOTT

A wonderfully balanced runner with a deceptive turn of pace and an unerring eye for a gap, Jeremy Guscott's performances for his hometown Bath soon made him a legend with the club's supporters and it wasn't long before England came calling. He made his international debut against Romania in Bucharest on 13 May 1989, scoring a hat-trick of tries (only Danny Lambert, with five against France in January 1907, has scored more on debut for England) in a 58–3 victory. Despite his relative inexperience at international level, Guscott was called up to the British Lions squad for the tour to Australia later that year, and made crucial contributions in both the second and third Tests as the Lions recorded their first series victory for 15 years.

With England, he forged an incisive centre partnership with captain Will Carling, and was a key member of the Grand Slam-winning team of 1991, and an integral part of the side that reached the Rugby World Cup final later in the year – scoring two tries in the tournament. He embarked on a second Lions tour in 1993, playing in all three Tests in New Zealand in the 2–1 series defeat, and although he missed much of the 1994 season through injury, he was an automatic selection for England's squad for Rugby World Cup 1995 in South Africa.

The tournament, at which Guscott failed to find his best form (even though England progressed to the semi-finals), signalled a turning point for both England and Guscott. After club-mate and fellow centre Phil de Glanville assumed the captaincy in 1996, Guscott found himself vying for the one remaining centre berth with Will Carling, and the Bath man often found himself on the bench – a decision Carling himself went on to describe in his autobiography as "extraordinary". But every time he came on, even if it was on the wing, he made a telling impact, particularly in England's victories over Ireland and Wales.

Despite his on-off appearances for England, the Lions came calling for a third time in 1997 for the tour against reigning world champions South Africa (notably both de Glanville and Carling were overlooked), and Guscott, dubbed the "Prince of Centres" by Clive Woodward, yet again played a crucial part in proceedings, landing a last-gasp drop-goal in the second Test in Durban to a secure an

England
Rugby

unassailable 2–0 series lead. Unfortunately for Guscott, the tour ended on a sour note when he broke his arm during the 35–16 defeat in the third and final Test in Johannesburg.

Guscott made the last of his 65 England appearances against Tonga at Rugby World Cup 1999 – typically, and to the great delight of the capacity Twickenham crowd, he marked the occasion by scoring a length-of-the-field interception try. It was his 30th try of a stellar international career – only three England players in history (Rory Underwood, Will Greenwood and Ben Cohen) have scored more.

FOR THE RECORD

Born	7 July 1965, Bath
Club	Bath (1984–2000)
England caps	65
Matches as captain	0
England points	143 (30 tries, 2 drop-goals)
British Lions Tests	8
British Lions points	7 (1 try, 1 drop-goal)
RWC appearances	13
RWC points	18 (4 tries)
Debut	v Romania, Bucharest, 13 May 1989
Last game	v Tonga, Twickenham, 15 October 1999

HONOURS

Five Nations titles	4 – 1991, 1992, 1995, 1996
Triple Crowns	6 – 1991, 1992, 1995, 1996, 1997, 1998
Grand Slams	3 – 1991, 1992, 1995
RWC honours	Runner-up – 1991
	Semi-finalist – 1995
	Quarter-finalist – 1999

Did You Know That?
Before his rugby career took off, Jeremy Guscott worked as a bricklayer and, briefly, as a bus driver.

MARTIN JOHNSON

Martin Johnson looked destined for greatness from the moment he first pulled on an England shirt. No less a rugby judge than New Zealand legend Colin Meads first spotted his potential, offering him the chance to play for King Country province in New Zealand. Johnson took up the offer, prospered, and went on to be capped by New Zealand Under-21. Many from New Zealand wished he had remained in the Land of the Long White Cloud, but Johnson returned and such a tough schooling would go on to serve both him and England well.

England coach Geoff Cooke came calling in 1993, propelling the 23-year-old Leicester lock straight into the starting XV as a late replacement for the injured Wade Dooley for England's Five Nations Championship clash against France. Johnson performed like a seasoned professional as England edged to a narrow 16–15 victory. It may have been his only appearance in that year's championship, but British Lions coach Ian McGeechan had seen enough to hand him a place on that year's tour to New Zealand. Johnson played in two of the three Tests, returning with his burgeoning reputation further enhanced.

Now a regular in the England starting XV, he won a first Grand Slam in 1995 and played every minute of every game at that year's Rugby World Cup in South Africa (at which England progressed to the semi-finals). It was McGeechan once again who helped propel Johnson's career upwards when he selected him as captain for the Lions' 1997 tour to South Africa. And when the Lions secured a 2–1 series victory, Johnson's place among the game's greats was already secure. Yet there was plenty more to come.

Coach Clive Woodward's appointment of Johnson to the role of captain, ultimately paved the way for the most successful period in England Rugby history. Where Woodward attended to every detail off the pitch, on the pitch Johnson provided an in-your-face, unyielding, never-say-die attitude the rest of his team-mates bought into – and the results were sensational.

England won the inaugural Six Nations Championship title in 2000, repeated the success in 2001, finished second behind France in 2002, and romped to Grand Slam glory in 2003 (the last time England have won the Grand Slam). Memorable victories over New

Zealand (15–13 in Wellington) and Australia (25–14 in Melbourne) later that summer saw England travel to = Rugby World Cup 2003 in Australia as the number-one-ranked team in the world and, along with New Zealand, the favourites to lift the trophy.

It was a status they lived up to. Helped in no small part by Jonny Wilkinson's unerring boot and Johnson's granite-like leadership, England marched through the tournament, beating Australia in a nerve-wracking final. It was thoroughly fitting that Johnson's final act in an England shirt was to become the first Englishman – and the only captain from the northern hemisphere – to lift the Webb Ellis trophy.

He returned to the England fold as coach in 2008, but could not emulate his feats as a player and resigned following the team's quarter-final exit at the Rugby World Cup 2011 in New Zealand.

FOR THE RECORD

Born	9 March 1970, Solihull
Club	Leicester Tigers (1989–2000)
England caps	84
Matches as captain	45
England points	10 (2 tries)
British Lions Tests	8
British Lions points	0
RWC appearances	18
RWC points	0
Debut	v France, Twickenham, 16 January 1993
Last match	v Australia, Sydney, 22 November 2003

HONOURS

Five/Six Nations titles	5 – 1995, 1996, 2000, 2001, 2003
Triple Crowns	6 – 1995, 1996, 1997, 1998, 2002, 2003
Grand Slams	2 – 1995, 2003
RWC honours	Winner – 2003
	Semi-finalist – 1995
	Quarter-finalist – 1999

JASON LEONARD

When Jason Leonard packed down for England for the first time, against Argentina in Buenos Aires on 28 July 1990, he became, at 17 days short of of his 22nd birthday, one England's youngest-ever forwards. Few thought the moment heralded the start of what would become the most decorated career in English rugby history. What was immediately clear, however, was that Leonard was made for international rugby.

A formidable scrummager and mobile in the loose, he quickly nailed down a place in England's starting XV, playing every match in both England's 1991 Grand Slam-winning campaign and their subsequent march to that year's Rugby World Cup final. A second Grand Slam followed in 1992 but, during England's Grand Slam-clinching victory over Wales, he ruptured a vertebra in his neck and required emergency surgery after the game. Remarkably, he was back in an England shirt later that autumn the next time they took to the field.

Leonard won his first two (of five) caps for the British Lions on their 1993 tour to New Zealand, was part of England's 1995 Grand Slam-winning team (during which he became England's most-capped prop), and appeared at his second Rugby World Cup later that year, as England reached the semi-finals.

He took to the onset of professionalism later that year in the same cool, clinical manner in which he had first taken to international rugby. He bulked himself up for the rigours of the game's new dawn and, crucially, learned to scrummage in both the loose- and tighthead positions – both changes undoubtedly added to his incredible longevity.

He survived Jack Rowell's post-Rugby World Cup cull (the new England coach vowed to end England's forward-oriented gameplan in favour of more open, running rugby) and was selected for his second Lions tour (to South Africa) in 1997. Still a cornerstone of the England pack, he played in his third Rugby World Cup in 1999, picked up further Six Nations honours in 2000 and 2001 (gaining selection for a third Lions tour, to Australia, in the latter year), and claimed the fourth Grand Slam of his career in 2003. During that tournament, against France at Twickenham, he became the first player in English rugby history to reach the 100-cap milestone.

Jason was part of Clive Woodward's Rugby World Cup 2003 squad and became the most capped player in international rugby when he won his 112th cap, against France in the semi-final (overtaking legendary centre Philippe Sella). Jason played a significant role when he came on as a replacement in the final, helping to stem the flow of penalties being awarded against the England scrum before Jonny Wilkinson drop-kicked the team to Rugby World Cup glory. He won the last of his 119 international caps against Italy in Rome in the 2004 RBS 6 Nations, and retired from the game a national legend.

FOR THE RECORD

Born	14 August 1968, Barking, London
Clubs	Saracens (1989–90), Harlequins (1990–2004)
England caps	114
Matches as captain	2
England points	5 (1 try)
British Lions Tests	5
British Lions points	0
RWC appearances	22
RWC points	0
Debut	v Argentina, Buenos Aires, 28 July 1990
Last match	v Italy, Rome, 15 February 2004

HONOURS

Five/Six Nations titles	7 – 1991, 1992, 1995, 1996, 2000, 2001, 2003
Triple Crowns	8 – 1991, 1992, 1995, 1996, 1997, 1998, 2002, 2003
Grand Slams	4 – 1991, 1992, 1995, 2003
RWC honours	Winner – 2003
	Runner-up – 1991
	Semi-finalist – 1995
	Quarter-finalist – 1999

Did You Know That?

Jason Leonard is now seventh in rugby's all-time appearances list. He is the third most-capped forward, after Richie McCaw (137 caps) and Victor Matfield (121) and most-capped prop.

RORY UNDERWOOD

Whatever Rory Underwood lacked in height (he stood just 5ft 9in tall), he more than made up for with an electric turn of speed. Born in Middlesbrough of English-Chinese heritage, he attended Barnard Castle School (alongside future England team-mate Rob Andrew) and steadily rose through the international ranks, appearing for England Students, England Colts, England Under-23s and England B before finally bursting on to the international scene, aged 20, in 1984.

An RAF Flight-Lieutenant off the pitch, he scored his first international try in only his second appearance, against France in Paris, providing England fans with a first glimpse of the searing speed that would become his trademark. Try-scoring opportunities proved elusive in that England side of that time, however, and by the time he returned from England's sobering Rugby World Cup 1987 campaign, he had scored only four tries in 19 appearances.

However, the arrival of Geoff Cooke as coach in 1988 marked a turning point both for England's rugby fortunes and for those of Underwood. That season, the Leicester wing scored nine tries in nine international appearances, and such form saw him selected for his first British Lions tour (the 1989 trip to Australia). He played in all three Tests as the Lions won the final match of the series to record a memorable 2–1 victory.

Now established as one of the most lethal finishers in world rugby, the tries continued to flow. Against Fiji at Twickenham in November 1989, he scored a then world record-equalling five tries in the match. He was part of England's Grand Slam-winning team in 1991 and was an ever-present in that year's Rugby World Cup (during which he won his 50th cap), scoring four tries as England fought their way to the final, only to lose out to Australia. He scored three tries in the 1992 Five Nations as England notched up a second successive Grand Slam and was joined in the starting XV by his younger brother Tony – the pair becoming the first siblings to play together in a match for England since Harold and Arthur Wheatley in England's 6–3 victory over Scotland in 1937.

He embarked on his second Lions tour (to New Zealand) in 1993, scoring the only try of his Lions career in the Lions' 32–15 victory in the second Test, although the series was ultimately lost. He picked up yet another Five Nations Grand Slam in 1995, and travelled to his third Rugby World Cup later that year – standing on the opposite wing as New Zealand's Jonah Lomu singlehandedly tore England's World Cup dreams to shreds.

The swansong finally came during the 1996 Five Nations Championship, and when Underwood bowed out of international rugby, following England's 28–15 victory over Ireland at Twickenham, he did so as England's all-time leading try-scorer. His tally of 49 tries (in 85 matches) is still the national record, 18 years after he made his final appearance, and it looks set to last for many more years.

FOR THE RECORD

Born	19 June 1963, Middlesbrough
Clubs	Leicester Tigers (1983–97)
	Bedford Blues (1998–99)
England caps	85
Matches as captain	0
England points	210 (49 tries)
British Lions Tests	6 – 1989, 1993
British Lions points	5 (1 try)
RWC appearances	15
RWC points	49 (11 tries)
Debut	v Ireland, Twickenham, 18 February 1984
Last match	v Ireland, Twickenham, 16 March 1996

HONOURS

Five Nations titles	4 – 1991, 1992, 1995, 1996
Triple Crowns	4 – 1991, 1992, 1995, 1996
Grand Slams	3 – 1991, 1992, 1995
RWC honours	Runner-up – 1991
	Semi-finalist – 1995
	Quarter-finalist – 1987

Did You Know That?
Rory Underwood stands sixth on international rugby's all-time try-scoring list – a true measure of his exceptional career.

WAVELL WAKEFIELD

One of the first posters boy of English rugby, Wavell Wakefield was known for his speed and athleticism on the pitch and is credited with revolutionizing the role of the back-row forward. Until he came along, back-row forwards chiefly had been restricted to set-piece play; Wakefield developed the idea of forward play in the loose, creating a defensive system that saw the open-side pressurizing the opposition fly-half from the set-piece. It is a role that is now customary for all who play in that position.

Affectionately known as "Wakers", he was educated at Sedburgh School, leaving during the First World War (in 1916) to join the Royal Naval Air Service and RAF (for which he attained the position of Flight-Lieutenant). He found the time during his stint with the Armed Forces to show his athleticism when he became the RAF's 440-yard dash champion. He joined Harlequins in 1919, and made his debut for England during their 19–5 defeat to Wales in Swansea on 17 January 1920, but better days lay ahead for both England and Wakefield.

He scored the first of his six international tries during England's hard-fought 14–11 victory over Ireland at Lansdowne Road later in the 1920 Five Nations Championship, and was an ever-present in England's Grand Slam-winning campaign the following year (the country's seventh). He captained Cambridge University in 1922–23 (he had continued his studies at Pembroke College), played a full part in England's Grand Slam-winning campaign in 1923 (scoring in their title-clinching victory over France at the Stade Colombes in Paris) and then assumed the captaincy from Dave Davies in 1924, leading England to only the second back-to-back Grand Slam in their history. He continued to lead his country until the end of the 1926 Five Nations campaign, before returning to the ranks for two matches of the 1927 Five Nations. His last match in an England shirt came against France at Stade Colombes on 2 April 1927 – a disappointing 3–0 defeat.

Wakefield continued to play for his beloved Harlequins until 1929, but remained in the public eye even after his retirement from playing. He went on to become the Conservative MP for Swindon (between 1935 and 1945) and later St Marylebone (between 1946 and 1963), was knighted in 1944, and on his retirement from

Parliament, in 1963, became the first Baron Wakefield of Kendal. He retained strong links with rugby too, serving as RFU President in 1950 and as President of the Harlequins from 1950 to 1980. In 1999, 16 years after his death (in 1983 aged 85), he was inducted as the first English member of the International Rugby Hall of Fame; it was due recognition of his contribution to the game both on and off the pitch.

FOR THE RECORD

Born	10 March 1898, Beckenham, Kent
Died	12 August 1983, Kendal, Cumbria
Club	Harlequins (1919–29)
England caps	31
Matches as captain	13
England points	18 (6 tries)
British Lions Tests	0
British Lions points	0
RWC appearances	0
RWC points	0
Debut	v Wales, Swansea, 17 January 1920
Last match	v France, Paris, 2 April 1927

HONOURS

Five Nations titles	4 – 1920, 1921, 1923, 1924
Triple Crowns	3 – 1921, 1923, 1924
Grand Slams	3 – 1921, 1923, 1924
RWC honours	None

Did You Know That?

Wavell Wakefield had several more strings to his bow. He was instrumental in establishing the Middlesex Sevens tournament for charity. An all-round sportsman, he also went on to serve as president of the Ski Club of Great Britain, the British Sub-Aqua Club and the British Water Ski Foundation. And his interests extended beyond the sporting arena, too. He also played a major role in preserving the Ravenglass and Eskdale Railway, that runs for seven miles through the Lake District in northern England.

JONNY WILKINSON

When Jonny Wilkinson landed that famous, last-gasp drop-goal against Australia in the Rugby World Cup 2003 final to secure the trophy for England, he secured not only a special place in the hearts of every England supporter, but also a place among the game's immortals.

The signs that he was a very special player were apparent from the moment he first pulled on an England shirt – against Ireland at Twickenham on 4 April 1988. In doing so, aged 18 years 314 days, he became England's second youngest debutant (only Colin Laird, against Wales at Twickenham in 1927 at 18 years 124 days was younger). He survived the team's disastrous "Tour of Hell" later that year (a 76–0 loss to Australia and 64–22 defeat to New Zealand). Although Jonny played in all of England's Five Nations Championship matches in 1999, when England played South Africa in the Rugby World Cup 1999 quarter-final, coach Clive Woodward named him only as a replacement. The match ended in disappointment for England in the form of a 44–21 defeat.

But being overlooked simply seemed to serve to make him work harder. Formidable in defence, relentless on the practice ground and unerring with the boot, he went on to make the England No.10 shirt his own. By the end of the 2001 Six Nations, still only 21 years of age, he had surpassed his mentor Rob Andrew's mark as England's all-time leading points-scorer. Later that year, he embarked on his first British Lions tour – a 2–1 series defeat to Australia, in which he played all three Tests. In 2002, he scored 21 and 22 points, respectively, as England recorded morale-boosting home wins over New Zealand and Australia, and then, in the 2003 RBS 6Nations, scored 77 points in the tournament as England romped to their first Grand Slam since 1995.

And then came Rugby World Cup 2003. But what should have served as a springboard for the man who had become the most revered fly-half on the planet merely served as a demoralizing turning point. Remarkably, as a series of debilitating injuries struck, 1,169 days would pass before Wilkinson reappeared in an England shirt. He overcame yet another injury scare on the eve of the tournament to play his part in England's unexpected march to the Rugby World Cup 2007 final, but was out-kicked on the day by

England
Rugby

South Africa's Percy Montgomery as England fell narrowly short. He also played under coach Martin Johnson during England's Rugby World Cup 2011 campaign, bowing out of international rugby at the end of the tournament with 1,179 points to his name – one of numerous national records he holds.

But if anyone thought that was the last you would hear of Jonny Wilkinson, they were mistaken. He had left Newcastle Falcons in 2009 for the sunnier Mediterranean climes of Toulon and, remaining largely injury-free, enjoyed a remarkable swansong to his career. Wilkinson won back-to-back European Cups with the French club in 2013 and 2014, retiring at the end of the latter campaign. He was still so good that he won the European Player of the Year award in 2013.

FOR THE RECORD

Born	25 May 1979, Frimley, Surrey
Clubs	Newcastle Falcons (1997–2009)
	Toulon (2009–14)
England caps	91
Matches as captain	2
England points	1,179 – 6 tries, 162 conversions, 239 penalties, 39 drop-goals
British Lions Tests	6
British Lions points	67 – 1 try, 7 conversions, 16 penalties
RWC appearances	19
RWC points	277 (1 try, 28 conversions, 58 penalties, 14 drop-goals)
Debut	v Ireland, Twickenham, 4 April 1998
Last match	v France, Auckland, 8 October 2011

HONOURS

Five/Six Nations titles	4 – 2000, 2001, 2003, 2011
Triple Crowns	3 – 1998, 2002, 2003
Grand Slams	1 – 2003
RWC honours	Winner – 2003
	Runner-up – 2007
	Quarter-finalist – 1999, 2011

England
Rugby

CHAPTER 3
ENGLAND'S GRAND SLAMS

There have been only 37 Grand Slams (victories over every opponent in a single Five/Six Nations Championship) in 120 editions of the famous tournament, and England lead the way with 12 of them – ahead of Wales (11), France (9), Scotland (3) and Ireland (2). This chapter tells the story of every one of England's memorable, and rare, Grand Slam seasons.

FIVE NATIONS CHAMPIONSHIP 1913

The Home Nations Championship began in 1883 and was played to a completion on 24 occasions before France joined the competition in 1910, creating the Five Nations Championship. Winning all three matches 1883–1909 was known as the Triple Crown – the four British unions against each other – but the Grand Slam became possible with France's arrival. Wales were the first to achieve it, in 1911, but England – Triple Crown winners in 1883, 1884 and 1892 – emulated the Grand Slam feat for the first time in 1913.

England's pre-tournament preparations consisted of a Test match against South Africa at Twickenham on 6 January 1913, and although they rang the changes, handing debuts to five players – most notably flying winger Cyril Lowe – a record-breaking crowd of 35,000 watched England suffer a 9–3 defeat, but it should be said that South Africa won 24 of their 27 matches on that tour (losing three). There were just 14 days for until the start of the Five Nations, however, and England knew they had work to do.

Even back in 1913, Cardiff was probably the most intimidating venue at which to open a tournament campaign. Wales were roared on by 20,000 passionate fans inside the National Stadium, but to no avail. England ran in two tries, through Vincent Coates and Robert "Cherry" Pillman, to record a 12–0 victory. It was the second successive year the mighty Welsh had failed to score a single point against England.

Next up for England were France at Twickenham. The French were still new to the Five Nations – winning only one match in their first three seasons – and had started their 1913 campaign with a heavy 21–3 defeat against Scotland. So, although England's 20–0 victory came as little surprise, the free-flowing nature of their game that day (they ran in six tries – three for Coates, two for Pillman and one for Ronald Poulton-Palmer) suggested the men in white had very much found their form. That notion was tested in England's next outing: an away trip to Dublin to face Ireland, the team with whom England had shared the championship in 1912. England outscored the Irish by four tries to nil (with two more scores for the impressive Coates) in a one-sided 15–4 victory and now found themselves just one win away from a coveted Grand Slam.

Remarkably, five weeks would pass between England's match against Ireland and their Grand Slam-deciding clash against Scotland at Twickenham: plenty of time for the level of anticipation to grow. A crowd of 25,000 crammed into Twickenham that day in the hope of witnessing a slice of history. England did not disappoint. Prop Bruno Brown scored the only try of the game in the first half as England held out for a nail-biting 3–0 victory. Their long wait for a Grand Slam was finally over.

RESULTS

Wales	0	**England**	12	Cardiff	18 Jan 1913
England	20	France	0	Twickenham	25 Jan 1913
Ireland	4	**England**	15	Lansdowne Road	8 Feb 1913
England	3	Scotland	0	Twickenham	15 Mar 1913

FINAL TABLE

Country	P	W	D	L	For	Against	Points
England	4	4	0	0	50	4	8
Wales	4	3	0	1	35	33	6
Scotland	4	2	0	2	41	28	4
Ireland	4	1	0	3	55	60	2
France	4	0	0	4	11	67	0

Captain	Norman Wodehouse
Most tries	Vincent Coates – 6
Most points	Vincent Coates – 18

Did You Know That?
England did not concede a single try during the 1913 Five Nations Championship, and remain the only team in the competition's history in all of its guises to have won a Grand Slam by conceding just a single score – a Dickie Lloyd drop-goal for Ireland during England's 15–4 victory at Lansdowne Road.

FIVE NATIONS CHAMPIONSHIP 1914

If England had been forced to climb the highest mountain to win a Grand Slam for the first time in 1913, they knew they would have to conquer a peak of Himalayan proportions if they were to repeat the feat in 1914. In the 30 years that had passed since the tournament's inception in 1883, only one side had won back-to-back Grand Slams – Wales, in 1908 and 1909.

England's opening game of the 1914 Five Nations, against Wales at Twickenham saw the team continue with Vincent Coates and Ronald Poulton-Palmer in their back division. They had dazzled in 1913. Wales, on the other hand, possessed the northern hemisphere's most fearsome pack, dubbed the "Terrible Eight" for their physical approach to the game. As it transpired, England's dash and verve won the day over Welsh brawn, with prop Bruno Brown (the try-scoring hero of England's Grand Slam-clinching victory over Scotland the previous year) and Charles "Cherry" Pillman crossing the line to secure a tense 10–9 victory that ensured the majority of the 30,000-strong crowd went home happy.

The win over Wales seemed to inspire the English rugby-watching public. Three weeks later, a crowd of 40,000 packed in to Twickenham for their next match against Ireland, among them King George V, who watched on from the Royal Box. Inspired perhaps by the presence of royalty, England put on a dazzling show, outscoring Ireland by five tries to two (two for Lowe and one each for Dave Davies, Pillman and Alan Roberts) en route to a 17–12 victory. England had overcome their two opening hurdles with aplomb.

A trip to Scotland has been the undoing of many of England's Grand Slam-winning aspirations over the years, and 1914 was ever so nearly another date to add to that lengthy list. Five weeks after their victory over Ireland, England had Cyril Lowe (with three tries) and Ronald Poulton-Palmer (with one) to thank as they recorded a narrow, nervy, 16–15 victory in Inverleith. England had completed the Triple Crown; all that stood between them and a historic, second-successive Grand Slam was a French team that had not won a single Five Nations match in ten attempts.

France did manage to put up a fight at the Stade Colombes on 13 April, scoring three tries, but they could not stop England. The visitors scored nine tries of their own – four for captain Poulton-Palmer, three for Lowe (taking his tournament haul to an all-time record eight), and one each for Davies and James "Bungy" Watson – as they romped to an easy 39–13 victory. For many involved that day, however, the Grand Slam celebrations would have been short-lived: within a matter of months, many of them would be fighting a very different battle on French soil – at the Western Front, at which a number of England's heroes that day would lose their lives.

RESULTS

England 10	Wales 9		Twickenham	17 Jan 1914
England 17	Ireland 12		Twickenham	14 Feb 1914
Scotland 15	**England** 16		Inverleith	21 Mar 1914
France 13	**England** 39		Colombes	13 Apr 1914

FINAL TABLE

Country	P	W	D	L	For	Against	Points
England	4	4	0	0	82	49	8
Ireland	4	3	0	1	29	34	6
Wales	4	2	0	2	75	18	4
Scotland	3	0	0	3	20	46	0
France	3	0	0	3	19	78	0

Captain	Ronald Poulton-Palmer
Most tries	Cyril Lowe – 8
Most points	Cyril Lowe – 24

Did You Know That?
Eleven of the 30 men who played in the 1914 Five Nations match between Scotland and England at Inverleith lost their lives during the First World War and nearly a quarter of the 116 players who participated in the nine championship matches that year were killed in action or died later from their wounds.

FIVE NATIONS CHAMPIONSHIP 1921

Of the 15 players who had lined up for England in their Grand Slam-clinching victory over France at Colombes on 13 April 1914, six lost their lives during the First World War: Arthur Dingle, Arthur Harrison, Francis Oakeley, Robert Pillman, captain Ronald Poulton-Palmer and James "Bungy" Watson. That, coupled with the natural passing of time, meant it was an enforced new-look England side that took to the field when the Five Nations Championship finally resumed in 1920. England won three out of four matches to share the championship with Wales and Scotland. In 1921, however, England were determined to go one better.

They got off to a blistering start, beating Wales (the only side to have beaten them in 1920) 18–3 at Twickenham, with Cecil Kershaw, Cyril Lowe (one of only three survivors from the 1914 Grand Slam-winning side, along with Bruno Brown, England's try-scoring hero in the 1913 Grand Slam-deciding match against Scotland, and Dave Davies) and Alastair Smallwood (with two tries) all crossing the line.

Four weeks later, an inexperienced Ireland side (featuring seven debutants) were Twickenham's next visitors, and a crowd of 27,500 were on hand to witness yet another convincing performance from the home team. Tries from Freddie Blakiston, Brown and Lowe handed England a 15–0 victory.

Trips to Inverleith to play Scotland had provided England with numerous stern challenges in the pre-war years, but not on this occasion. England dominated the match, scoring four tries (one each for Brown, Reg Edwards, debutant Quentin King and Tom Woods) in a one-sided and thoroughly convincing 18–0 victory.

As had been the case in 1914, a trip to play France at the Stade Colombes in Paris, stood between England and Grand Slam glory. Unlike in 1914, however, this was a fast-improving French side (one that had won two of its three matches going into the clash), and England would have to be at their very best to win. It was a game that captured the public's imagination. Thousands flocked to the stadium, with many of the spectators breaking down the barricades to gain access to the ground, and it took the intervention of mounted police, who were forced to line the perimeter of the pitch, before the match could get under way.

England
Rugby

None of this seemed to affect England, however. They scored the only two tries of the game, through Arthur Blackiston and the prolific Lowe, to secure a 10–6 victory and the third Grand Slam in their history. Nobody was to know it at the time, but it was the start of what would turn out to be a golden period for English rugby – the most prolific era in the side's illustrious history, with four Grand Slams in eight years.

RESULTS

England	**18**	Wales	3	Twickenham	15 Jan 1921
England	**15**	Ireland	0	Twickenham	12 Feb 1921
Scotland	0	**England**	**18**	Inverleith	19 Mar 1921
France	6	**England**	**10**	Colombes	28 Mar 1921

FINAL TABLE

Country	P	W	D	L	For	Against	Points
England	4	4	0	0	61	9	8
France	4	2	0	2	33	32	4
Wales	4	2	0	2	29	36	4
Scotland	4	1	0	3	22	38	2
Ireland	4	1	0	3	19	49	2

Captain	Dave Davies
Most tries	Cyril Lowe – 3
Most points	Cyril Lowe – 13

Did You Know That?
England's +52 points difference during the 1921 Grand Slam-winning campaign was their best to date, surpassing the +46 difference of 1913. In fact, it stood as England's record for 69 years until they finished the 1990 campaign with a points difference of +64 when there were four points for a try and three for a drop-goal.

FIVE NATIONS CHAMPIONSHIP 1923

England were the Five Nations Championship's dominant force in the early 1920s. They had collected four consecutive titles in the years immediately preceding and following the First World War (collecting three Grand Slams along the way – in 1913, 1914 and 1921), but their defence of the trophy in 1922 had got off to a disapponting – and, ultimately, championship-losing – start when they suffered a 28–6 defeat to Wales in Cardiff (their biggest reverse since going down 22–0 to the same opponents at Swansea in 1901). Wales went on to claim the 1922 Championship, with England (who also drew 11–11 at home to France) finishing in second place. All of which made England's desire to make amends in 1923 all the greater.

England's chance to gain revenge over the reigning champions came in the opening round of matches in the Five Nations Championship. And they edged a closely contested affair at Twickenham. Flanker Leo Price scored for England; Gwilym Michael crossed the line for Wales; but an Alastair Smallwood drop-goal (the only one of his international career and worth four points under the old scoring system) ultimately proved the difference between the two sides. England won the game 7–3 and celebrated the win knowing they had overcome their first, and arguably most significant, hurdle.

England travelled to Leicester's Welford Road stadium for their second match to host an Ireland side in sharp decline. And the home side lived up to their favourite's tag with aplomb, thrilling the 20,000-strong crowd by running in five tries – one each for Len Corbett, Cyril Lowe, Smallwood, Price and Tom Voyce – in a convincing and one-sided 23–5 victory.

A trip to Inverleith to play Scotland did not hold the same fear for England as it might have done in times gone by. England had emerged victorious on their last two trips to Edinburgh's northern suburb (in 1914 and 1921), and made it three wins out of three thanks to a hard-fought 8–6 victory, with Smallwood and Voyce scoring England's tries, with further points coming from the boot of William Luddington.

As had been the case so often in the past, England would have to beat France at the Stade Colombes to complete the Grand Slam. It might only have been a sign of the times (or perhaps an indication of England's supreme confidence), but their Welsh-born captain, fly-half and talisman Dave Davies chose the occasion to take his new bride on honeymoon to the French capital.

England added to his mood of celebration by winning 12–3 thanks to tries from Geoffrey Conway and rising star Wavell Wakefield, with Davies contributing a drop-goal. England had won the Grand Slam for the fourth time in their history and for the second time in three seasons.

RESULTS

England	7	Wales	3	Twickenham	20 Jan 1923
England	23	Ireland	5	Leicester	10 Feb 1923
Scotland	6	England	8	Inverleith	17 Mar 1923
France	3	England	12	Colombes	2 Apr 1923

FINAL TABLE

Country	P	W	D	L	For	Against	Points
England	4	4	0	0	50	17	8
Scotland	4	3	0	1	46	22	6
Wales	4	1	0	3	31	31	2
France	4	1	0	3	28	52	2
Ireland	4	1	0	3	21	54	2

Captain   Dave Davies
Most tries   Leo Price, Alastair Smallwood,
                     Tom Voyce – 2
Most points   Alastair Smallwood – 10

Did You Know That?
Having achieved the feat in both 1914 and 1921, 1923 would be the third and final time England clinched a Grand Slam on French soil. In fact, of the eight further Grand Slams England would go on to win, only two of them were clinched away from Twickenham – at Murrayfield in 1980 and at Lansdowne Road in 2003.

FIVE NATIONS CHAMPIONSHIP 1924

The 1924 Five Nations campaign was a bit of a leap into the
unknown for England as, for the first time since 1913, they entered
the tournament without the services of long-standing fly-half and
recent captain Dave Davies. The No.10 had been a talisman for this
England side. Remarkably, he had only lost once in an England shirt
in 22 appearances – on debut against South Africa in 1913. Davies
had been injured when England travelled to Cardiff to play in Wales
1922, and the 22–0 defeat ended any chance of winning a Grand
Slam. Davies had called time on his international career following
England's 1923 Grand Slam-clinching victory over France. Firebrand
flanker Wavell Wakefield had taken over as captain, and England
did not have to wait too long to find out just how badly they might
miss their former captain. Their opening match of the 1924 Five
Nations Championship was against Wales in Swansea.

Maybe it was because the match was not played in Cardiff (and
all of the bad memories that venue would have evoked for this
England side), or perhaps it was simply an indication of just how
far the side had come, but the visitors gave the 35,000-strong
crowd that had packed into the St Helen's ground nothing to
shout about on 19 January 1924. Wales may have run in three tries
of their own that day, but England ran in five – two for debutant
Carston Catcheside and one each for Jake Jacob (another
debutant), Harold Locke and Edward Myers – in a surprisingly one-
sided 17–9 victory.

England then travelled to Belfast to face Ireland, who had beaten
France 6–0 in their opening match – the first time the men in green
had opened a Five Nations campaign with a victory since 1914.
And, buoyed by their win against the French, the Irish held their
own in the first half, going into the interval with the scores locked
at 3–3. It was a different story in the second half, however. England
found their stride, ran in three tries to silence the 15,000-strong
Ravenhill crowd and recorded a 14–3 victory.

With two games remaining, England could start to dream of a
third Grand Slam in four years, particularly given their opponents.
In the 13 matches England had played against France to that point,
they had won 12 of them and drawn once, scoring 283 points and
conceding a mere 68. Their home record against Scotland was

equally impressive: the Scots had last tasted success on English soil way back in 1907. In short, given the way England were playing, they would have approached their final two games of the campaign with supreme confidence.

And it showed. On 23 February 1924, they proved too strong for France, delighting the 40,000-strong Twickenham crowd by scoring five tries in a 19–7 victory. And Scotland proved no match for England three weeks later: roared on by a record 45,000 crowd eager to witness a slice of history, England scored three tries – through Catcheside, Myers and captain Wakefield – in a 19–0 win. England had recorded back-to-back Grand Slams for only the second time in their history and this one (their fifth), had perhaps been the most impressive of them all.

RESULTS

Wales	9	**England**	17	Swansea	19 Jan 1924
Ireland	3	**England**	14	Belfast	9 Feb 1924
England	19	France	7	Twickenham	23 Feb 1924
England	19	Scotland	0	Twickenham	15 Mar 1924

FINAL TABLE

Country	P	W	D	L	For	Against	Points
England	4	4	0	0	69	19	8
Scotland	4	2	0	2	58	49	4
Ireland	4	2	0	2	30	37	4
France	4	1	0	3	25	45	2
Wales	4	1	0	3	39	71	2

Captain	Wavell Wakefield
Most tries	Carston Catcheside – 6
Most points	Carston Catcheside – 18

England Rugby

FIVE NATIONS CHAMPIONSHIP 1928

The sustained period of dominance many had expected to see
from England after the men in white had won three Grand Slams in
four years (1921, 1923 and 1924) failed to materialize. They finished
second behind Scotland in 1925 – losing 14–11 at Murrayfield in their
final game to hand the Scots a first-ever Grand Slam. It was even
more disappinting in 1926 as England won only once and finished
fourth in the Five Nations.

A year later, after captain Wavell Wakefield had retired, England
were third, and lost to France in the tournament for the first time.
Thus expectations were not high as England embarked on their
1928 Five Nations campaign – even though they had recorded a
morale-boosting 18–11 victory over Australia at Twickenham just
two weeks before the tournament got under way with a side
featuring five debutants.

England were scheduled to open their campaign against
Wales in Swansea. In recent times, the Principality had not been
the graveyard for English hopes it had been in the pre-First
World War years; indeed, the last time England had crossed the
Severn Bridge they had emerged with a 3–3 draw. They went
one better on this occasion, scoring two tries (through William
Kirwan-Taylor and 19-year-old Colin Laird) to emerge with a
hugely creditable 10–8 victory. The surprising victory meant
that England could look forward to the rest of the campaign with
renewed confidence.

They travelled to Lansdowne Road, Dublin, three weeks later to
play Ireland, and once again found a way of dragging themselves
across the winning line. The hosts may have outscored England
by two tries to one (with centre James Richardson scoring
England's only try), but a Richardson drop-goal ultimately
proved the difference between the two sides as England returned
home across the Irish Sea celebrating a 7–6 victory. Against all
the odds, England had won their opening two fixtures of the
campaign, and with two home matches remaining, they could
dare to dream.

It also seemed as though the English public had started to
believe too. A massive crowd of 70,000 turned out to see England
take on France at Twickenham two weeks after their victory over

Ireland. And England, eager to avenge the defeat in Paris the previous year and riding on the crest of their renewed confidence, gave their vociferous supporters plenty to shout about. Godfrey Palmer and Joe Periton scored two tries apiece as England recorded a 18–8 victory. This all meant that England would take on Scotland in the final match of the tournament gunning for a Grand Slam.

And what a tense affair it turned out to be at Twickenham as England scored a try in each half of a nail-biting encounter (through Jerry Hanly and Laird) to win the match 6–0. It was England's sixth Grand Slam, and their most surprising one, but few of the thousands gathered at Twickenham that day would have thought that 29 years would pass before England would have the chance to celebrate such an occasion again.

RESULTS

Wales	8	**England**	10	Swansea	21 Jan 1928
Ireland	6	**England**	7	Lansdowne Road	11 Feb 1928
England	18	France	8	Twickenham	25 Feb 1928
England	6	Scotland	0	Twickenham	17 Mar 1928

FINAL TABLE

Country	P	W	D	L	For	Against	Points
England	4	4	0	0	41	22	8
Ireland	4	3	0	1	44	30	6
Wales	4	1	0	3	34	31	2
Scotland	4	1	0	3	20	38	2
France	4	1	0	3	30	48	2

Captain Ron Cove-Smith
Most tries Colin Laird, Godfrey Palmer,
Joe Periton – 2
Most points James Richardson – 17

FIVE NATIONS CHAMPIONSHIP 1957

To dismiss England's achievements in the years following their sixth Grand Slam success in 1928 through to the mid-1950s as years of underachievement would be to ignore the fact that those years contained many highlights. Grand Slam success may have eluded England – but it did for most teams. Remarkably, only three Grand Slams were won between 1929 and 1956, by Ireland in 1948 and by Wales in 1950 and 1952. However, as France were excluded from the championship after 1931 and World War 2 halted the tournament 1940–46, it meant that only the Triple Crown could be won between 1932 and 1939: a feat England achieved in 1934 and 1937. But in England, dreams of a seventh Grand Slam continued to grow, particularly given that the side had come so close to one a number of times in the early 1950s. And, in 1957, it all came right for England.

They started their campaign with a trip to play reigning champions Wales in Cardiff. England had made four visits to the Welsh capital since the tournament resumed in 1947 (with France back in the competition), winning two and losing two. Notably, however, every one of those matches had been tough, low-scoring affairs, with never more than six points separating the two sides. And so it proved again, with Coventry full-back Fenwick Allison's first-half penalty proving the difference between the two sides as England did enough to record a 3–0 victory.

Buoyed by their win over the Welsh, England crossed the Irish Sea to take on Ireland at Lansdowne Road, Dublin. It was a venue that yielded few good memories for England supporters; they had not seen their side win there since 1938. But this was turning out to be a different England side, and a try from Coventry wing Peter Jackson, coupled with a penalty from debutant full-back Bob Challis, handed England a 6–0 victory. With two home games remaining, English expectations were starting to grow.

A crowd of 60,000 packed into Twickenham on 23 February 1957 to watch England's first home match, against France. The French were no longer the tournament's poor relations, having shared the championship title for the first time in 1954 and again the following year, but they proved no match for England on this occasion, as tries from captain Eric Evans and Jackson (two) saw the home side to a 9–5 victory.

All that stood between England and Grand Slam glory was a Scotland side also gunning for the title. The Scots had lost their opening game against Ireland, but successive victories had left them with their own shot at glory – and the Scots would have liked nothing more than to derail England's dream in their own backyard. It wasn't to be for Scotland, however: England ran in three tries to none en route to a surprisingly comfortable 16–3 victory. The long wait was over: England had won a Grand Slam for the first time in 39 years.

RESULTS

Wales	0	**England**	3	Cardiff	19 Jan 1957
Ireland	0	**England**	6	Lansdowne Road	9 Feb 1957
England	9	France	5	Twickenham	23 Feb 1957
England	16	Scotland	3	Twickenham	16 Mar 1957

FINAL TABLE

Country	P	W	D	L	For	Against	Points
England	4	4	0	0	34	8	8
Wales	4	2	0	2	31	30	4
Ireland	4	2	0	2	21	21	4
Scotland	4	2	0	2	21	27	4
France	4	0	0	4	24	45	0

Captain	Eric Evans
Most tries	Peter Jackson – 3
Most points	Bab Challis – 10

Did You Know That?
In the build-up to England's game against Scotland, a reporter from The Times *had coined a phrase to describe a team who had managed to win every one of their Five Nations Championship matches – the term "Grand Slam" entered the rugby lexicon for the first time.*

FIVE NATIONS CHAMPIONSHIP 1980

England's decline did not begin straight after their 1957 Grand Slam success. They won the title again in 1958, shared the championship with France in 1960 and claimed the title outright in 1963 (denied a Grand Slam only by a 0–0 draw against Ireland in Dublin). There was also the statistical oddity of the 1973 competition when all five teams won their two home matches, so the title – before points difference was a tie-breaker – was shared five ways. But in the 1970s, in particular, all was not well with English rugby, and by the end of the 1979 campaign (in which they had finished fourth), they had not won more than two matches in a tournament since 1963.

There was, however, some cause for hope. In November 1979, a North of England XV, captained by Bill Beaumont and containing the likes of Mike Slemen, John Carleton, Steve Smith, Fran Cotton, Roger Uttley and Tony Neary, had beaten the legendary All Blacks 21–9. And when the stars of that team were merged with the standout performers from England's leading club side at the time, Leicester Tigers, miraculous things started to happen.

England opened their 1980 Five Nations campaign in pulsating style against Ireland at Twickenham. Tries from No.8 John Scott, wing Slemen and scrum-half Smith, coupled with 12 points from the boot of full-back Dusty Hare, handed them a comfortable, and unexpected, 24–9 victory.

England needed every ounce of the confidence gained by their victory over the Irish as they crossed the Channel to take on France in Paris. England had not won in the French capital for 16 years, and when the two sides had met at the Parc des Princes two years earlier, England had been on the receiving end of a 30–9 defeat. Not on this occasion: England stood toe-to-toe with the French, with tries from wing Carleton and centre Nick Preston, two John Horton drop-goals and a Hare penalty enough to hand them a narrow 17–13 victory. However, an even sterner challenge lay ahead.

Wales, the reigning Five Nations champions, had been the great side of the 1970s, claiming the title on seven occasions and bagging three Grand Slams in the process. They had won their opening match against France comfortably (18–9) and expected more of the same against England, particularly given that they had emerged victorious in their last two visits to Twickenham.

England
Rugby

It was not an attractive game to watch and Welsh flanker Paul Ringer was sent off following a high tackle on Horton. But three Hare penalties – including the match-winner in the dying seconds of the game – were enough to edge England to a memorable 9–8 victory.

With a first Grand Slam in 23 years now firmly within their grasp, England travelled to Murrayfield as firm favourites to beat Scotland. And they lived up to the tag by producing a superb performance, scoring five tries (three for Carleton and one each for Slemen and Smith) in a comfortable 30–18 victory.

RESULTS

England 24	Ireland 9		Twickenham	19 Jan 1980
France 13	**England 17**		Parc des Princes	2 Feb 1980
England 9	Wales 8		Twickenham	16 Feb 1980
Scotland 18	**England 30**		Murrayfield	15 Mar 1980

FINAL TABLE

Country	P	W	D	L	For	Against	Points
England	4	4	0	0	80	48	8
Ireland	4	2	0	2	70	65	4
Wales	4	2	0	2	50	45	4
France	4	1	0	3	55	75	2
Scotland	4	1	0	3	61	83	2

Coach	Mike Davis
Captain	Bill Beaumont
Most tries	John Carleton – 4
Most points	Dusty Hare – 34

Did You Know That?
The 80 points England scored during the 1980 Grand Slam-winning campaign had been bettered only once before – in 1914, when the team scored 82 points to win the Grand Slam.

England Rugby

FIVE NATIONS CHAMPIONSHIP 1991

If winning a Grand Slam is the measure that distinguishes a good side from a great one, then England under coach Geoff Cooke and captain Will Carling still had some way to go as they embarked on their 1991 Five Nations campaign. The pair had masterminded an astonishing upturn in England's fortunes – the low point had come when they finished the 1987 Championship with the Wooden Spoon – to title challengers. But the big prize still eluded them – disappointingiy so in 1990 when they had travelled to Murrayfield to play Scotland in a Grand Slam decider as firm favourites and fell to a 13–7 defeat. So England had plenty to prove in 1991 – doubly so, given that a Rugby World Cup on home soil was just around the corner.

If England were keen to make an early statement of intent, they were handed the perfect opportunity to do so in their opening game against Wales in Cardiff – a city in which they had not won since 1963. They scored the only try of the match, through Mike Teague, and that, coupled with a remarkable seven penalties from the boot of full-back Simon Hodgkinson, was enough to see them to a comfortable 25–6 victory. England had finally broken the Cardiff hoodoo, and they were up and running.

Next they were handed a chance to exact revenge on the Scotland side that had snatched the Grand Slam from their grasp the previous year – this time, though, at Twickenham. And there was to be no Scottish cheer on this occasion: winger Nigel Heslop scored the game's only try and Hodgkinson picked up where he had left off in Cardiff, slotting five penalties and a conversion, as England won 21–12.

They were strong favourites to beat Ireland at Lansdowne Road, too. Ireland, having lost one and drawn one of their opening two games, had plenty to prove and, roared on by a vociferous home crowd, held England to 3–3 at half-time. But England's forward power finally told in the second half, and tries from Teague and Rory Underwood helped them to a 16–7 victory.

This set up a winner-takes-all, Grand Slam-deciding clash (the second in two years but only the fourth ever) against France at Twickenham. And what a match it turned out to be: the French outscored England by three tries to one (from Underwood), but, as had been the case throughout the tournament, Hodgkinson's boot proved to be England's most potent weapon. The full-back landed four penalties and a conversion as England edged to a 21–19 victory. The Grand Slam that had so narrowly eluded them the year before was finally theirs, and this England side was now on the verge of becoming a great one.

RESULTS

Wales	6	**England** 25	Cardiff	19 Jan 1991
England 21	Scotland	12	Twickenham	16 Feb 1991
Ireland	7	**England** 16	Lansdowne Road	2 Mar 1991
England 21	France	19	Twickenham	16 Mar 1991

FINAL TABLE

Country	P	W	D	L	For	Against	Points
England	4	4	0	0	83	44	8
France	4	3	0	1	91	46	6
Scotland	4	2	0	2	81	73	4
Ireland	4	0	1	3	66	86	1
Wales	4	0	1	3	42	114	1

Coach	Geoff Cooke
Captain	Will Carling
Most tries	Mike Teague, Rory Underwood – 2
Most points	Simon Hodgkinson – 60

Did You Know That?
Statistically, at least, England's 1991 Grand Slam-clinching campaign pales in comparison with their efforts of the previous year. They scored fewer points (83 in 1991, 90 in 1990), fewer tries (five as opposed to 12) and conceded more points (44 compared to 26). The major difference, of course, was that they won all their matches in 1991.

FIVE NATIONS CHAMPIONSHIP 1992

Even though England had claimed a first Grand Slam for 11 years in 1991, there was still a feeling the side had something to prove going into the 1992 Five Nations. Only months before the tournament began, their forward-oriented approach to the game had seen them reach the Rugby World Cup final, only for them to throw caution – and seemingly their gameplan – to the wind in what had been the biggest game of their lives and come up short, losing 12–6 to Australia. So the question on everyone's lips as the 1992 Five Nations got under way was which England would turn up: a forward-dominated XV or a free-flowing one? As it turned out, it was a combination of the two and it proved to be unstoppable. In fact, so dominant were England that their narrowest margin of victory was 18 points.

England opened their campaign against Scotland at Murrayfield – the scene of the two sides' epic Rugby World Cup semi-final only months before. But whereas that had been an understandably cagey affair (with England winning 9–6 and Scotland left to rue Gavin Hastings' late missed penalty from virtually under the posts), this match was a far more fluid affair. England led 10–7 at the interval before holding the Scots pointless in the second half. England scored tries through Dewi Morris and Rory Underwood; Jonthan Webb kicked a conversion and four penalties and Jeremy Guscott added a drop-goal as they ran out 25–7 winners.

Next England faced Ireland at Twickenham, and they produced a brilliant display of attacking rugby. They dominated Ireland, running in six tries – two for Webb (whose first came after a mere 24 seconds and he finished the match with 22 points) and one each for Guscott, Simon Halliday, Morris and Underwood – in what turned out to be a comprehensive 38–9 victory.

Full of confidence, England crossed the Channel to take on France at the Parc des Princes. Four months earlier, the two teams had met at the same venue in the Rugby World Cup quarter-finals, with England coming out on top. And although that match was one of the competition's most fiercely contested games, it was outdone in this disappointingly hard fixture. The match, at times, bore little resemblence to international rugby, but England kept their heads and, more importantly, their discipline while the French lost theirs (two players, Gregoire Lascube and Vincent Moscato, were sent off) and emerged from the penalty-strewn contest with a 31–13 win, scoring four tries – from Morris, Underwood, Webb (who also booted 15 points) and a penalty try – in the process.

England returned to a more placid Twickenham for their final match of the tournament, against Wales, knowing a place in the history books was up for grabs. And the result was never in doubt from the moment Will Carling collected a speculative Rob Andrew kick to cross the line in the opening minutes of the game. Mickey Skinner and Wade Dooley (playing in his 50th and final match for England) also crossed the line as England ran out 24–0 winners. They had won back-to-back Grand Slams for the first time since 1923–24.

RESULTS

Scotland	7	**England** 25	Murrayfield	18 Jan 1992
England 38		Ireland 9	Twickenham	1 Feb 1992
France	13	**England** 31	Parc des Princes	15 Feb 1992
England 24		Wales 0	Twickenham	7 Mar 1992

FINAL TABLE

Country	P	W	D	L	For	Against	Points
England	4	4	0	0	118	29	8
France	4	2	0	2	75	62	4
Scotland	4	2	0	2	47	56	4
Wales	4	2	0	2	40	63	4
Ireland	4	0	0	4	46	116	0

Coach	Geoff Cooke
Captain	Will Carling
Most tries	Dewi Morris, Rory Underwood, Jonathan Webb – 3
Most points	Jonathan Webb – 67

FIVE NATIONS CHAMPIONSHIP 1995

Following their back-to-back Grand Slam successes in 1991 and 1992, it was always going to be difficult for England to maintain such sustained excellence. And so it proved. They won only two of their four matches in 1993, losing 10–9 to Wales in Cardiff and 17–3 to Ireland in Dublin, and lost to Ireland again in 1994, this time at Twickenham, and had to settle for second place in the championship. But beyond the Five Nations, England still showed they were a force to be reckoned with on the world stage, beating New Zealand 15–9 at Twickenham in November 1993 and, more significantly, beating South Africa 32–15 in Pretoria in June 1994. With a Rugby World Cup looming later in the year, and now playing under new coach Jack Rowell, the 1995 Five Nations was an opportunity for England to reassert their dominance over their northern hemisphere neighbours.

They opened their campaign with a trip to Lansdowne Road and a chance to avenge the defeat to the Irish two years earlier. And England overcame both the passionate home crowd and the inclement weather to win the match 20–8, with captain Will Carling, Ben Clarke and Tony Underwood (the younger brother of Rory) scoring the tries.

A return to Twickenham to play France lay in wait for England. The French had not won in London since 1987 and never looked like ending that losing streak. England dominated the match, with Jeremy Guscott and Tony Underwood (two) running in the tries and Rob Andrew adding 16 points with the boot (four penalties and two conversions) in a one-sided 31–10 victory.

Two weeks later, England were handed another opportunity to banish bad memories from 1993 when they travelled to Cardiff to play Wales. And, as had been the case in their opening two matches, the match against the Welsh proved to be another one-sided affair. England scored the only tries of the match, through prop Victor Ubogu and Tony Underwood (with two), Rob Andrew added another eight points with the boot, and ran out comfortable 23–9 winners – only once (in 1991) had England's margin of victory in Cardiff been higher.

Victory over Wales started to bring back memories of 1990 all over again. England would face unbeaten Scotland in the final

England
Rugby

round of matches, with the title, the Grand Slam, the Triple Crown and the Calcutta Cup all at stake for the victor. This time, however, the match would be played at Twickenham. Maybe the enormity of the occasion got the better of both teams, but the match turned out to be a dour, nervy affair, with Rob Andrew (seven penalties and a drop-goal) outkicking his Scottish counterparts to hand England a hugely efficient 24–12 victory. It may not have been their most stylish performance of the campaign, but it mattered not: England had won their third Grand Slam in five years.

RESULTS

Ireland	8	**England 20**	Lansdowne Road	21 Jan 1995
England 31		France 10	Twickenham	4 Feb 1995
Wales	9	**England 23**	Cardiff	18 Feb 1995
England 24		Scotland 12	Twickenham	18 Mar 1995

FINAL TABLE

Country	P	W	D	L	For	Against	Points
England	4	4	0	0	98	39	8
Scotland	4	3	0	1	87	71	6
France	4	2	0	2	77	70	4
Ireland	4	1	0	3	44	83	2
Wales	4	0	0	4	43	86	0

Coach	Geoff Cooke
Captain	Will Carling
Most tries	Tony Underwood – 3
Most points	Rob Andrew – 53

Did You Know That?
The 1995 Five Nations Championship was the last to be held in rugby union's amateur era. The sport officially turned professional on 26 August 1995.

RBS 6 NATIONS CHAMPIONSHIP 2003

From 2000, England – under coach Clive Woodward and captain Martin Johnson – started to make giant strides towards becoming one of world rugby's leading teams. They had taken a number of impressive scalps: beating South Africa 27–22 in Bloemfontein on 24 June 2000; edging to a 31–28 victory over New Zealand at Twickenham on 9 November 2002; and very easily beating South Africa 53–3, also at headquarters, on 23 November 2002. But Six Nations Grand Slam glory continued to elude them. They had come close, winning the championship in 2000 and 2001, but on both occasions had fallen just short at the final hurdle – losing 19–13 to Scotland at Murrayfield in the former and to Ireland, 20–14 at Lansdowne Road, in the latter. England were determined to get everything right in 2003.

They made a great start against reigning champions France at Twickenham. France outscored England by three tries to one (Jason Robinson scoring for England), but the home side showed glimpses of the formula that would lead them to Rugby World Cup glory later in the year: be patient and pressure the opponent into making mistakes and conceding penalties in the knowledge that they had the best goal-kicker in world rugby. Jonny Wilkinson kicked five penalties, a conversion and a drop-goal as England won 25–17.

Next England travelled to the Millennium Stadium in Cardiff to play Wales. This stadium held fond memories for England: their only previous visit, in 2001, had seen them win 44–15. The winning margin may not have been as big on this occasion, but the manner of England's performance was equally impressive. Will Greenwood and Joe Worsley scored the tries, and Wilkinson added 16 points with his left boot in a comfortable 26–9 victory.

England treated the Twickenham fans to a try-fest against Italy two weeks later. Josh Lewsey (twice), Dan Luger, James Simpson-Daniel, Steve Thompson and Mike Tindall all crossed the line as England cruised to a 40–5 win. And it was more of the same against Scotland, too. England scored four tries in the match – through Robinson (two), Ben Cohen and Lewsey – on the way to a comfortable 40–9 victory.

As had been the case in 2001, all that stood between England and Grand Slam glory was a trip to Lansdowne Road, Dublin, to play

Ireland. But if memories of that painful defeat were still raw, England soon dispelled them. They simply dominated the Irish, scoring five tries without reply – through Lawrence Dallaglio, Greenwood (two), Luger and Tindall – in a thoroughly impressive 42–6 victory. The Grand Slam was finally England's. The only trophy missing from this team's trophy cabinet was the Rugby World Cup – and they would claim that eight months later.

RESULTS

England 25	France 17		Twickenham	15 Feb 2003
Wales 9	**England** 26	Millennium Stadium	22 Feb 2003
England 40	Italy 5		Twickenham	9 Mar 2003
England 40	Scotland 9		Twickenham	22 Mar 2003
Ireland 6	**England** 42		Lansdowne Road	30 Mar 2003

FINAL TABLE

Country	*P*	*W*	*D*	*L*	*For*	*Against*	*Points*
England	5	5	0	0	173	46	10
Ireland	5	4	0	1	119	97	8
France	5	3	0	2	153	75	6
Scotland	5	2	0	3	81	161	4
Italy	5	1	0	4	100	185	2
Wales	5	0	0	5	82	144	0

Coach	Clive Woodward
Captain	Will Carling
Most tries	Will Greenwood, Josh Lewsey,
	Jason Robinson – 3
Most points	Jonny Wilkinson – 77

Did You Know That?

The 46 points conceded by England in 2003 is the fewest by any team in the in the 16 seasons of teh Six Nations Championship.

England
Rugby

CHAPTER 4
ENGLAND IN THE RUGBY WORLD CUP

One of only 11 teams to have appeared at all seven editions of the Rugby World Cup since the tournament's inception in 1987, England have enjoyed both dizzying highs and devastating lows in the competition. This chapter tells the story of every one of England's performances on the game's greatest stage.

RUGBY WORLD CUP 1987

The idea of a Rugby World Cup had first been mooted back in the 1950s, only to be met with widespread opposition from most of the International Rugby Board's (IRB) members, but when the IRB announced that the inaugural Rugby World Cup would take place in Australia and New Zealand in May and June 1987, the news was met with widespread joy among rugby supporters around the world – finally, after more than a century of international rugby, they would have the chance to see a side become the undisputed champions of world rugby.

For England, however, the inaugural Rugby World Cup could not have come at a worse time. In the years building up to the tournament, the national team had been on a disappointing run, finishing fourth in the 1985 Five Nations, equal third in 1986, and picking up the wooden spoon in 1987 only months before the tournament was due to begin (with only one victory, against Scotland, to their name). Only the most optimistic of England fans could have expected the team to produce any extended run in the competition.

And so it proved. England, captained by Wakefield wing Mike Harrison, started their Rugby World Cup story against joint hosts and pre-tournament favourites Australia at the Concord Oval in Sydney. They lost full-back Marcus Rose to severe concussion just five minutes into the match and went on to lose 19–6 without ever really hitting their stride. Given the side's form in the build-up to the tournament, however, it could only be described as an encouraging performance, and if England could muster wins against their other two Pool One opponents, which they were expected to do, they would still progress to the tournament's knockout stages.

They found some measure of form against Japan, running in ten tries (with Harrison scoring three of them and Leicester wing Rory Underwood two) en route to a convincing 60–7 victory. And, four days later, they also proved too strong for the United States, scoring four tries (two for flanker Peter Winterbottom and one each for Harrison and lock Wade Dooley) as a 34–6 victory secured them a place in the last eight.

Wales, who had topped their group following victories over Ireland, Tonga and Canada, lay in wait for them in the quarter-finals.

When the two sides had met earlier in the year, in the Five Nations in Cardiff, Wales had edged a hard-fought match 19–12, but any England fans hoping for a similarly close encounter this time round would be left disappointed. Wales dominated the match, scoring three tries to none in a comprehensive 16–3 victory – and England's hopes of making a big impact at the inaugural Rugby World Cup were over. Although England may have gone home early, they learned quickly from their mistakes.

FOR THE RECORD

Coach	Martin Green
Captain	Mike Harrison
Results	v Australia, lost 6–19 (pool)
	v Japan, won 60–7 (pool)
	v United States, won 34–6 (pool)
	v Wales, lost 3–16 (quarter-final)
Leading try-scorer	Mike Harrison (5)
Leading points-scorer	Jonathan Webb (43)

SQUAD

Backs: Rob Andrew (Wasps); Mark Bailey (Wasps); Fran Clough (Orrell); Jon Hall (Bath); Richard Harding (Bristol); Mike Harrison (Wakefield, captain); Richard Hill (Bath); Marcus Rose (Harlequins); Jamie Salmon (Harlequins); Kevin Simms (Wasps); Rory Underwood (RAF/Leicester); Peter Williams (Orrell); Jonathan Webb (Bristol)

Forwards: Steve Bainbridge (Fylde); Gareth Chilcott (Bath); Graham Dawe (Bath); Wade Dooley (Fylde); David Egerton (Bath); Brian Moore (Nottingham); Nigel Redman (Bath); Gary Rees (Nottingham); Dean Richards (Leicester); Gary Pearce (Northampton); Jeff Probyn (Wasps); Paul Rendall (Wasps); Peter Winterbottom (Headingley)

Did You Know That?
England averaged 3.75 tries per match during the Rugby World Cup 1987, beating their returns in 1991 (1.83), 1995 (1.83) and 2007 (1.71).

RUGBY WORLD CUP 1991

As disappointing as their Rugby World Cup 1987 campaign had been, it also proved something of a watershed moment for the England rugby team. Geoff Cooke was appointed team manager in October 1987, and after seeing his charges finish third in the 1988 Five Nations Championship (recording two wins), decided the time was ripe to ring the changes. In came Will Carling as captain and, on 5 November 1988, England's bright new era kicked off with a memorable 28–19 victory over Australia at Twickenham. All of a sudden, it appeared as though England's supporters had a team worth shouting about.

England finished second in the 1989 Five Nations and repeated that showing in 1990 (famously denied both the Grand Slam and the title by Scotland at Murrayfield), before romping to the Grand Slam (the ninth of England's history and their first in 11 years) in 1991. And so it was with great confidence that England embarked on their Rugby World Cup 1991 campaign – even more so given they would play the majority of their matches on home soil.

Their credentials were tested in the opening match of the tournament – against defending champions New Zealand at Twickenham. And although they led 12–9 at half-time (thanks to three Jonathan Webb penalties and a Rob Andrew drop-goal), a second-half try from Michael Jones saw New Zealand edge to an 18–12 victory.

England recovered well from their opening-game setback, recording a 36–6 victory over Italy and a 37–9 win over the United States, but the consequence of their defeat to the All Blacks now became apparent. England would have to face France in Paris in the quarter-finals. In the passionate atmosphere of the Parc des Princes, England held their nerve and tries from Rory Underwood and Carling were enough to secure a 19–10 victory. Next up were Scotland at Murrayfield, and a chance to exact revenge for that 1990 Grand Slam defeat. In what turned out to be a very cagey match – not surprising given the prize at stake – England won 9–6. They had made it to the Rugby World Cup 1991 final the hard way: next in line were Australia at Twickenham.

But there was to be no repeat of that glorious victory in the autumn of 1988 on this occasion. England, perhaps forced by the

England
Rugby

additional pressure of winning the tournament as hosts, decided to abandon the forward-oriented style that had proved to be so successful on their road to the final, in favour of a more attacking approach.

It did not pay dividends: Australia scored the only try of the match, through prop Tony Daly after 28 minutes, and their defence held firm in the face of countless England attacks to hold out for a 12–6 victory. An England side playing mighty close to the peak of its powers had come up just a little bit short.

FOR THE RECORD

Coach	Geoff Cooke
Captain	Will Carling
Results	v New Zealand, lost 12–18 (pool)
	v Italy, won 36–6 (pool)
	v United States, won 37–9 (pool)
	v France, won 19–10 (quarter-final)
	v Scotland, won 9–6 (semi-final)
	v Australia, lost 6–12 (final)
Leading try-scorer	Rory Underwood (4)
Leading points-scorer	Jonathan Webb (56)

SQUAD

Backs: Rob Andrew (Wasps); Will Carling (Harlequins, captain); Jeremy Guscott (Bath); Simon Halliday (Bath); Nigel Heslop (Orrell); Richard Hill (Bath); Simon Hodgkinson (Nottingham); Dewi Morris (Orrell); Chris Oti (Wasps); David Pears (Harlequins); Rory Underwood (RAF/Leicester); Jonathan Webb (Bath)

Forwards: Paul Ackford (Harlequins); Wade Dooley (Fylde); Jason Leonard (Harlequins); Brian Moore (Harlequins); John Olver (Northampton); Gary Pearce (Northampton); Jeff Probyn (Wasps); Nigel Redman (Bath); Gary Rees (Nottingham); Paul Rendall (Wasps); Dean Richards (Leicester); Mickey Skinner (Harlequins); Mike Teague (Gloucester); Peter Winterbottom (Harlequins)

RUGBY WORLD CUP 1995

If England considered the Rugby World Cup 1991 as the one that had slipped through their fingers, then the 1995 edition of the tournament turned out to be the one in which their hopes of lifting the trophy for the first time were simply blown away by a force of nature they simply could not control.

England had retained much of the core of the team that had reached the final in 1991, with Will Carling continuing in his role as captain, alongside old hands Rory Underwood and Rob Andrew in the backs, and Dean Richards and Brian Moore in the pack. There had been a change in coach, with Jack Rowell taking over from Geoff Cooke in 1994 – the former Bath coach promising to deliver a more attacking England team.

The post-Rugby World Cup 1991 hangover had not lasted long either. England had bounced back from the disappointment of losing the final to win the Five Nations Grand Slam in 1992, had finished second (behind a resurgent Wales) in 1994, and travelled to South Africa for the fourth edition of the Rugby World Cup off the back of a third Grand Slam in five years – their status as the best team in the northern hemisphere undisputed.

All of which made their disappointing start to the tournament so surprising. Far from their free-flowing best, they had Rob Andrew to thank after his six penalties and two drop-goals handed them a nervy 24–18 victory over Argentina (who had outscored England by two tries to none). And it was a similar story against Italy: both sides scored two tries (the Underwood brothers, Rory and Tony, grabbing one each for England), but Andrew outkicked *Azzurri* counterpart Diego Dominguez (17 points to ten) to help England to a welcome, but narrow, 27–20 victory. A 44–20 win against Samoa in the final round of pool matches signalled a return to some sort of try-scoring form, but England knew they would have to raise their game if they were to overcome defending champions Australia – their conquerors in the 1991 final – in the quarter-final in Cape Town.

It was an epic match. England led 13–6 at half-time thanks to a Tony Underwood try, but with 82 minutes on the clock, the scores were locked at 22–22. England won a lineout on the Australian 10-metre line, they caught the ball, drove towards the Australian 22, scrum-half Dewi Morris passed to Andrew, and the England No.10 nailed the drop-goal attempt to hand England a 25–22 victory.

New Zealand and the overall player of the tournament, Jonah Lomu, lay in wait for England in the semi-final. England could find no answer to the 6ft 5in winger, who scored three tries inside the first 20 minutes to render the contest effectively over by half-time. England rallied in the second half, scoring twice through Carling and Rory Underwood, but the 45–29 scoreline reflected the All Blacks' superiority. And a few days later, England lost their third-place playoff game against France, 19–9.

FOR THE RECORD

Coach	Jack Rowell
Captain	Will Carling
Results	v Argentina, won 24–18 (pool)
	v Italy, won 27–20 (pool)
	v Samoa, won 44–20 (pool)
	v Australia, won 25–22 (quarter-final)
	v New Zealand, lost 29–45 (semi-final)
	v France, lost 9–19 (third-place playoff)
Leading try-scorer	Rory Underwood (5)
Leading points-scorer	Rob Andrew (79)

SQUAD

Backs: Rob Andrew (Wasps); Kyran Bracken (Bristol); Mike Catt (Bath); Jonathan Callard (Bath); Phil de Glanville (Bath); Ian Hunter (Northampton); Will Carling (Harlequins, captain); Jeremy Guscott (Bath); Damian Hopley (Wasps); Tony Underwood (Leicester); Rory Underwood (Leicester)

Forwards: Neil Back (Leicester); Martin Bayfield (Northampton); Ben Clarke (Bath); Graham Dawe (Bath); Martin Johnson (Leicester); Jason Leonard (Harlequins); John Mallett (Bath); Brian Moore (Harlequins); Steve Ojomoh (Bath); Dean Richards (Leicester); Tim Rodber (Northampton); Graham Rowntree (Leicester); Victor Ubogu (Bath); Richard West (Gloucester)

RUGBY WORLD CUP 1999

The history books suggest that the Rugby World Cup 1999 was a tournament too soon for England, but it's hard to believe that is what coach Clive Woodward and his men were thinking at the time. For while it may be true that England had undergone something of a rebuilding process since Rugby World Cup 1995 – stalwarts such as Will Carling, Rob Andrew, Rory Underwood and Brian Moore had long since hung up their international boots – a new generation of excellent players, under the leadership of Martin Johnson, had made their own mark.

They had won Five Nations Triple Crowns (albeit not the championship) in both 1997 and 1998, and had come very close to winning the Grand Slam in 1999, only to be denied by a last-gasp Scott Gibbs try that handed Wales a 32–31 victory at Wembley. In short, the titles might not have come their way, but there must have been a feeling within the England camp that they were on the verge of something special and that Rugby World Cup 1999 would have provided them with the perfect platform to prove it.

England opened their campaign, against Italy at Twickenham, in style, running in eight tries en route to a comfortable 67–7 victory. The match was notable for the performance of fly-half Jonny Wilkinson, who contributed 32 points to England's haul. Next up were New Zealand – and as had been the case eight years earlier, the All Blacks would provide a far more realistic yardstick against which to measure England's tournament credentials. New Zealand outscored England by three tries to one in a comfortable 30–16 victory, and England, it seemed, were some way short of being able to compete with the very best.

They rounded out their Pool B matches with an easy, 13-try, 101–10 victory over Tonga, but the major consequence of their defeat to the All Blacks was that they had to enter a playoff round to win a place in the quarter-finals. England ultimately beat Fiji 45–24, but it meant they had played one more match than their last-eight opponents, reigning champions South Africa, and no one really knew what effect that would have on the outcome of the match. Probably even more crucially than having played a game more, England went into the quarter-final on only four days' rest, while South Africa had not played for more than a week.

Exhaustion may have been a factor as England lost at the Stade de France, but the bottom line was that South Africa were the better team on the day. Fly-half Jannie de Beer produced the game of his life, nailing a world record five drop-goals and that, coupled with tries from Joost van der Westhuizen and Pieter Roussow, was enough to see South Africa enjoy a 44–21 victory.

FOR THE RECORD
Coach Clive Woodward
Captain Martin Johnson
Results v Italy, won 67–7 (pool)
v New Zealand, lost 16–30 (pool)
v Tonga, won 101–10 (pool)
v Fiji, won 45–24 (quarter-final playoff)
v South Africa, lost 44–21 (quarter-final)
Leading try-scorer Dan Luger (4)
Leading points-scorer Jonny Wilkinson (69)

SQUAD
Backs: Nick Beal (Northampton); Kyran Bracken (Saracens); Mike Catt (Bath); Matt Dawson (Northampton); Phil de Glanville (Bath); Paul Grayson (Northampton); Will Greenwood (Leicester); Jeremy Guscott (Bath); Austin Healey (Leicester); Dan Luger (Saracens); Matt Perry (Bath); David Rees (Sale); Jonny Wilkinson (Newcastle)

Forwards: Gareth Archer (Newcastle); Neil Back (Leicester); Richard Cockerill (Leicester); Martin Corry (Leicester); Lawrence Dallaglio (Wasps); Darren Garforth (Leicester); Phil Greening (Sale); Richard Hill (Saracens); Martin Johnson (Leicester, captain); Jason Leonard (Harlequins); Neil McCarthy (Gloucester); Danny Grewcock (Saracens); Tim Rodber (Northampton); Graham Rowntree (Leicester); Victor Ubogu (Bath); Phil Vickery (Gloucester); Joe Worsley (Wasps)

Did You Know That?
Rugby World Cup 1999 was the only one to have a quarter-final playoff round

RUGBY WORLD CUP 2003

England found themselves in unusual territory as they headed off to Australia for the Rugby World Cup 2003. Whereas in previous tournaments they had merely been hopeful of success, on this occasion, nothing less than tournament victory would do. Over-confidence? Not this time.

England's progress in the years building up to the tournament had been hugely impressive: they had won an RBS 6 Nations Grand Slam in 2003, beaten Australia, New Zealand and South Africa at home and, just four months before the tournament, recorded impressive away victories over both New Zealand (15–13 in Wellington) and Australia (25–14 in Melbourne). They boasted the strongest pack in world rugby and in fly-half Jonny Wilkinson its best goal-kicker (both would prove pivotal to their success). By the time the England squad boarded the plane to Australia they were ranked the No.1 side in the world and were considered joint favourites (alongside New Zealand) to lift the Webb Ellis trophy.

England showed top form in their opening game, running in 12 tries (with two each for Ben Cohen and Will Greenwood) in an 84–6 defeat of Georgia. They laid down a statement of intent in their next match, beating South Africa 25–6, with Wilkinson contributing 20 points and England advanced without fuss in their remaining pool matches – beating Samoa (35–22) and Uruguay (111–13) – knowing that sterner challenges lay ahead.

But for a while against Wales, in the quarter-final at Brisbane, it seemed as though England were fallible. The Welsh led 10–3 at half-time, before a vastly improved second-half performance saw a England record a 28–17 victory. They weren't at their free-flowing best against France in the semi-final either, but this was an England team that had learned how to win when not everything was going their way. The French scored the only try of the match, but the unerring boot of Wilkinson proved the difference between the two sides – the fly-half kicking all of England's points in a 24–7 victory.

And so to the final, against Australia in Sydney. The Wallabies took an early lead when Lote Tuqiri gathered a cross-field kick ahead of Jason Robinson to cross the line, before three Wilkinson penalties and a Robinson try saw England take a 14–5 half-time lead. But Australia bounced back in the second half, and by the end of

80 minutes, the scores were tied at 14–14. Extra-time proved nerve-wracking: both sides scored penalties, to make it 17–17. And then came the most famous moment in England's rugby history. England won a lineout, Matt Dawson broke into Australia's 22, the ball was recycled, England drove again, and then Dawson fed Wilkinson, who landed a drop-goal from 30 metres. England had edged into a 20–17 lead and Australia had no time to reply. It was mission accomplished for England: they had become champions of the world.

FOR THE RECORD

Coach	Clive Woodward
Captain	Martin Johnson
Results	v Georgia, won 84–6 (pool)
	v South Africa, won 25–6 (pool)
	v Samoa, won 35–22 (pool)
	v Uruguay, won 111–13 (pool)
	v Wales, won 28–17 (quarter-final)
	v France, won 24–7 (semi-final)
	v Australia, won 20–17 (final)
Leading try-scorers	Will Greenwood, Josh Lewsey (5)
Leading points-scorer	Jonny Wilkinson (113)

SQUAD

Backs: Stuart Abbott (Wasps); Iain Balshaw (Bath); Kryan Bracken (Saracens); Mike Catt (Bath); Ben Cohen (Northampton); Matt Dawson (Northampton); Andy Gomarsall (Gloucester); Paul Grayson (Northampton); Will Greenwood (Harlequins); Josh Lewsey (Wasps); Dan Luger (Perpignan); Jason Robinson (Sale); Mike Tindall (Bath); Jonny Wilkinson (Newcastle)

Forwards: Neil Back (Leicester); Martin Corry (Leicester); Lawrence Dallaglio (Wasps); Danny Grewcock (Bath); Richard Hill (Saracens); Martin Johnson (Leicester, captain); Ben Kay (Leicester); Jason Leonard (Harlequins); Lewis Moody (Leicester); Mark Regan (Leeds); Simon Shaw (Wasps); Steve Thompson (Northampton); Phil Vickery (Gloucester); Dorian West (Leicester); Julian White (Leicester); Trevor Woodman (Gloucester); Joe Worsley (Wasps)

RUGBY WORLD CUP 2007

By the time the Rugby World Cup 2007 came around, the glories of 2003 seemed a distant memory for the vast majority of England fans. The world champions had endured a disappointing run since that memorable night in Sydney. They had not finished higher than third in four RBS 6 Nations campaigns, were effectively playing under a new coach (Brian Ashton was only nine months into the job by the time England headed to France), and, remarkably, a long string of injuries had kept the team's talisman, Jonny Wilkinson, out of international action for the best part of three years. England's mercurial fly-half may have returned for the 2007 RBS 6 Nations campaign, but the invincible aura he once possessed now seemed to be one of vulnerability.

The possibility that England might find it difficult in the tournament became apparent from their performance in their opening game. They may have recorded a 28–10 victory over the United States, but it was a scoreline that flattered England, who never really took control of a match they were expected to win easily. Even worse news for England was that Wilkinson had suffered a sprained ankle before the match, and doubts remained as to whether he would be able to play any part in the tournament at all, let alone in England's next pool match – a crucial encounter against South Africa.

England's defeat of the United States was comfortable enough, 28–10, but the loss to South Africa in Paris in the next was a big disappointment. The Springboks beat England 36–0; it was their record defeat in a Rugby World Cup match and the first time they had failed to score a single point in an international for 19 years. It left England needing to beat Samoa and Tonga respectively to have any chance of progressing to the quarter-finals. With fit-again Wilkinson back in the fold, they did just that, recording 44–22 and 36–20 victories to set up a quarter-final clash against Australia.

And, for a short while, it seemed like 2003 all over again. Australia took the lead through a Lote Tuquiri try, before England's pack finally took control of the game and four Wilkinson penalties handed them a 12–10 victory. They proved too strong for France in the semi-finals too, a Josh Lewsey try coupled with two Wilkinson penalties and a drop-goal enough to see them to a 14–9 victory. Few would have believed it possible five weeks earlier, but, remarkably,

England had progressed to their second-successive Rugby World Cup final – against their pool group conquerors, South Africa. There was to be no repeat of 2003 on this occasion, however. In what turned out to be a hard-fought, closely contested, tryless affair, South Africa kicked five penalties to England's two for a 15–6 victory. England's extraordinary journey ended so close to history.

FOR THE RECORD

Coach	Brian Ashton
Captain	Phil Vickery
Results	v United States, won 28–10 (pool)
	v South Africa, lost 0–36 (pool)
	v Samoa, won 44–22 (pool)
	v Tonga, won 36–20 (pool)
	v Australia, won 12–10 (quarter-final)
	v France, won 14–9 (semi-final)
	v South Africa, lost 6–15 (final)
Leading try scorer	Paul Sackey (4)
Leading points-scorer	Jonny Wilkinson (67)

SQUAD

Backs: Nick Abendanon (Bath); Olly Barkley (Bath); Mike Catt (London Irish); Mark Cueto (Sale); Andy Farrell (Saracens); Toby Flood (Newcastle); Andy Gomarsall (Harlequins); Dan Hipkiss (Leicester); Josh Lewsey (Wasps); Jamie Noon (Newcastle); Shaun Perry (Bristol); Jason Robinson (unattached); Peter Richards (London Irish); Paul Sackey (Wasps); Mathew Tait (Newcastle); Jonny Wilkinson (Newcastle)

Forwards: Steve Borthwick (Bath); Martin Corry (Leicester); George Chuter (Leicester); Lawrence Dallaglio (Wasps); Nick Easter (Harlequins); Perry Freshwater (Perpignan); Ben Kay (Leicester); Lee Mears (Bath); Lewis Moody (Leicester); Tom Rees (Wasps); Mark Regan (Bristol); Simon Shaw (Wasps); Andrew Sheridan (Sale); Matt Stevens (Bath); Phil Vickery (Wasps, captain); Joe Worsley (Wasps)

RUGBY WORLD CUP 2011

Heartened in no small part by their surprise run to the Rugby
World Cup 2007 final, it was business as usual for England as
they embarked on their 2008 RBS 6 Nations campaign. But when
they won only three of their five matches (losing to Wales and,
surprisingly, to Scotland), it was felt a change of direction was
needed. Out went Brian Ashton as coach as England turned to
Martin Johnson, hoping the Rugby World Cup-winning captain
could inspire his charges to the higher reaches of world rugby once
again – albeit this time in an off-the-field capacity.

Initially, at least, the change in coach appeared to do little to arrest
England's mixed fortunes. They finished second in the 2009 RBS 6
Nations and third in 2010, but when they ended the 2011 campaign
as champions (just six months short of the Rugby World Cup 2011),
there was a sense the team had turned a corner. England supporters
dared to dream that their side, yet again, could have some impact
on the tournament. Significantly, however, the men in white had
recorded only two victories in 12 attempts over the southern
hemisphere rivals (Australia, New Zealand and South Africa) since
Rugby World Cup 2007. The optimists may not have wanted to
believe it, but, despite the obvious progress England had made, they
still appeared unable to compete with the very best in the world.
And so it would prove when the squad ventured to New Zealand.

England kicked off their campaign with a battling 13–9 victory
over Argentina in what turned out to be a bruising encounter in
Dunedin – a second-half try from replacement scrum-half Ben
Youngs proving the difference between the two sides. England had
the opening victory they craved, but with Argentina missing six
penalty attempts during the match, they must have known they had
been fortunate to do so.

They produced a second-half blitz to dismiss the challenge of
Georgia in their next match, running in six tries en route to a 41–10
victory. And they continued in the same try-scoring vein against
Romania six days later, this time running in ten tries in a convincing
67–3 victory – a game that saw both Mark Cueto and Chris Ashton
score hat-tricks. But signs all was not well with England emerged
in their final pool match against Scotland in Auckland. The Scots
dominated the first half and held a deserved 9–3 lead at the interval;

it took an improved second-half performance, and a 77th-minute try from Chris Ashton, to see England to a 16–12 win. England had achieved their first goal and progressed to the quarter-finals.

The last-eight match against France was effectively over at half-time, as tries from Vincent Clerc and Maxime Medard saw the French race into a 16–0 lead. England rallied in the second half, but it was too little too late: they lost the match 19–12, and their tournament dreams were over.

FOR THE RECORD

Coach	Martin Johnson
Captain	Lewis Moody
Results	v Argentina, won 13–9 (pool)
	v Georgia, won 41–10 (pool)
	v Romania, won 67–3 (pool)
	v Scotland, won 16–12 (pool)
	v France, lost 12–19 (quarter-final)
Leading try-scorer	Chris Ashton (6)
Leading points-scorer	Chris Ashton (30)

SQUAD

Backs: Delon Armitage (London Irish); Chris Ashton (Northampton); Matt Banahan (Bath); Mark Cueto (Sale); Toby Flood (Leicester); Ben Foden (Northampton); Shontayne Hape (London Irish); Joe Simpson (Wasps); Mike Tindall (Gloucester); Manu Tuilagi (Leicester); Richard Wigglesworth (Saracens); Jonny Wilkinson (Toulon); Ben Youngs (Leicester)

Forwards: Dan Cole (Leicester); Alex Corbisiero (London Irish); Tom Croft (Leicester); Louis Deacon (Leicester); Nick Easter (Harlequins); Dylan Hartley (Northampton); James Haskell (Ricoh Black Rams); Courtney Lawes (Northampton); Lee Mears (Bath); Lewis Moody (Leicester, captain); Tom Palmer (Stade Francais); Simon Shaw (Toulon); Matt Stevens (Saracens); Steve Thompson (Wasps); Thomas Waldrom (Leicester); David Wilson (Bath); Tom Wood (Northampton)

England
Rugby

CHAPTER 5
ENGLAND'S FAMOUS RUGBY COACHES

England had been playing international rugby for 98 years before, in 1969, they finally appointed their first coach – the former international Don White. Fourteen coaches have since followed, with some enjoying considerably more success in the role than others. Here's a look at a selection of the England team's standout coaches.

GEOFF COOKE

He may have been a promising player in his own right, captaining both his club (Bradford RFC) and county (Cumbria), but it is for his role as England head coach that Geoff Cooke will be best remembered. Under his regime, England went from being pretenders to champions, achieving the first consecutive Grand Slams in the Five Nations since the 1920s, and reaching a Rugby World Cup final.

Cooke's appointment as England head coach came in October 1987 following what had been a disappointing campaign at the inaugural Rugby World Cup. In truth, however, the World Cup display had come as little surprise: England had not enjoyed success for years, the glory of the 1980 Grand Slam was a distant, all-but-faded memory. Cooke led England to third place in the 1988 Five Nations – and then decided to ring the changes.

His appointment of Will Carling as captain for England's opening match of the 1988 autumn internationals, against Australia at Twickenham, suprised many, but it proved to be a masterstroke. Carling, just 22 years old at the time, had played in a mere seven internationals, but he showed his leadership as England recorded a memorable 28–19 victory, and produced a performance that prompted former Wallaby Michael Lynagh to say, "That was the day England got serious at rugby union."

England finished second in both the 1989 and 1990 Five Nations, but stormed to the title in 1991 (landing their ninth Grand Slam in the process). As a result, England entered the Rugby World Cup 1991 as genuine contenders for the title.

And how close they came; England came out on top in epic battles against France (in the quarter-finals) and Scotland (in the semi-finals) before narrowly falling short against Australia in the final (12–6). Five Nations honours continued to come their way, however, as they marched to a second-successive Grand Slam in 1992, before their form dipped in 1993 as they lost to both Wales (9–10) and Ireland (3–19).

And then came the bombshell. On 28 February 1994, even though he was contracted to the end of the Rugby World Cup 1995 campaign, Cooke announced that he would be resigning from the position at the end of the 1994 Five Nations, citing the need to spend more time both with his family and on his business. No one knew how great a loss it might prove to English rugby; the team had, after all, flourished under his control, winning 36 games, losing 13 and drawing one and, notably, had recorded victories against every one of the game's major rugby-playing nations. Cooke will always be remembered as the man who turned England into one of the strongest teams in world rugby.

FOR THE RECORD

Born	11 June 1941
Span as coach	16 January 1988–19 March 1994
Record as coach	Played – 49; Won – 35; Drawn – 1; Lost – 13
Win % as coach	71.43%
Honours as coach	Five Nations (1991, 1992)

ENGLAND'S PERFORMANCE UNDER COOKE

Team	Mat	W	L	D	Win %	PF	PA	Diff
Argentina	3	2	1	0	66.66	89	27	+62
Australia	5	1	4	0	20.00	73	121	-48
Canada	1	1	0	0	100.00	26	13	+13
Fiji	3	3	0	0	100.00	111	47	+64
France	8	7	1	0	87.50	151	88	+63
Ireland	8	6	2	0	75.00	164	62	+102
Italy	1	1	0	0	100.00	36	6	+30
New Zealand	2	1	1	0	50.00	27	27	0
Romania	1	1	0	0	100.00	58	3	+55
Scotland	8	6	1	1	81.25	124	82	+42
South Africa	1	1	0	0	100.00	33	16	+17
USA	1	1	0	0	100.00	37	9	+28
Wales	7	4	3	0	57.14	119	53	+66

Did You Know That?

Geoff Cooke was the first England coach to lead his side to victories over Australia (once – 28-19 in 1988), New Zealand (once – 15-9 in 1993) and South Africa (once – 33-16 in 1992) – all of the wins were at Twickenham.

SIR CLIVE WOODWARD

When Jack Rowell resigned as England coach in August 1997, there was hardly a long queue of candidates waiting to take over the job. Leading contenders Bob Dwyer (who had taken Australia to Rugby World Cup success in 1991) and Richard Hill (the former England scrum-half who was enjoying a successful stint as Gloucester coach) both ruled themselves out of the running, and, in the end, the RFU turned to Clive Woodward, the former England and British Lions centre, who was enjoying some measure of success as coach of the England Under-21 set-up. It was an appointment that would ultimately lead England to the very top of the rugby tree.

Not that such heady heights seemed likely in the early years of his regime. The Woodward era got off to an inauspicious start with a draw against Australia, followed by three defeats (two against New Zealand and one against South Africa). England then finished second in the 1998 Five Nations, before embarking on a tour to the southern hemisphere later that summer that would hit the headlines for all the wrong reasons. Dubbed the "Tour of Hell", England lost every match they played – notably a 76–0 defeat to Australia in Brisbane.

England narrowly missed out on a Grand Slam in the 1999 Five Nations, but still embarked on that year's Rugby World Cup campaign with hope. Before the tournament, Woodward had told the assembled press to judge him on his team's performances in the competition, so when England exited at the quarter-final stage following a comprehensive defeat to South Africa, the knives were out for him. Woodward kept his job, however, and every England fan would be grateful that he did.

For rather than breaking the England team, the disappointment of Rugby World Cup 1999 arguably made them. They won the inaugural Six Nations title in 2000 (although they fell short of the Grand Slam after a narrow defeat to Scotland at Murrayfield), but showed just how far they had come by beating South Africa 27–22 in Bloemfontein later that summer (their first victory against a southern hemisphere opponent since 1995). What followed was a sequence of almost unprecedented success: another Six Nations title in 2001; home victories over New Zealand, South Africa and Australia in 2002; a Grand Slam in 2003; followed by an historic

15–13 victory over New Zealand in Wellington later that summer. By the start of the Rugby World Cup 2003, England were the No.1 ranked team in world rugby. And they justified the hype, marching through the tournament to become the first team from the northern hemisphere to lift the Webb Ellis trophy. Success earned Woodward a knighthood. He decided to stay on as England coach after the World Cup, but when England failed to reach the same lofty heights, he resigned in the autumn of 2004.

FOR THE RECORD

Born	6 January 1956
Span as coach	15 November 1997–2 September 2004
Record as coach	Played – 83; Won – 59; Drawn – 2; Lost – 22
Win % as coach	71%
Honours as coach	Rugby World Cup (2003);
	Six Nations (2000, 2001, 2003)

ENGLAND'S PERFORMANCE UNDER WOODWARD

Team	Mat	W	L	D	Win %	PF	PA	Diff
Argentina	2	2	0	0	100.00	45	18	+27
Australia	10	5	4	1	55.00	176	272	-96
Canada	3	3	0	0	100.00	117	41	+76
Fiji	1	1	0	0	100.00	45	24	+21
France	10	6	4	0	60.00	247	161	+86
Georgia	1	1	0	0	100.00	84	6	+78
Ireland	7	5	2	0	71.42	226	106	+120
Italy	7	7	0	0	100.00	364	80	+284
Netherlands	1	1	0	0	100.00	110	0	+110
New Zealand	9	2	6	1	27.77	143	298	-155
Romania	1	1	0	0	100.00	134	0	+134
Samoa	1	1	0	0	100.00	35	22	+13
Scotland	7	6	1	0	85.71	218	88	+130
South Africa	10	6	4	0	60.00	217	173	+44
Tonga	1	1	0	0	100.00	101	10	+91
Uruguay	1	1	0	0	100.00	111	13	+98
USA	2	2	0	0	100.00	154	27	+127
Wales	9	8	1	0	88.88	359	151	+208

MARTIN JOHNSON

When, in April 2008, those in charge of English rugby came to the conclusion that Brian Ashton was not the man to lead England back to the top of world rugby, they turned to Martin Johnson. The former England captain had no coaching experience, but it was hoped that his sheer presence and standing in the game would inspire all those who played for him – just as it had done when he led England to success in the Rugby World Cup 2003 final.

He officially took over the reins for England's opening game of the 2008 autumn internationals, a 39–13 victory over the Pacific Islanders, but the size of the task he faced became apparent when his new charges slumped to successive defeats against Australia (28–14), South Africa (42–6) and New Zealand (32–6). But rather than hit the panic button, Johnson decided against ringing the changes for the 2009 RBS 6 Nations campaign. His faith was rewarded with a convincing 36–11 opening victory against Italy. Back-to-back away defeats to Wales (23–15) and Ireland (14–13), however, dashed any hopes England might have had of winning the championship, and although they finished with home victories over France (34–10) and Scotland (26–12), a second-place finish in the final table hardly represented the start of a bright new era everyone had been hoping for.

And they continued in much the same vein throughout 2009, recording a pair of home victories over Argentina before falling to morale-sapping home losses to Australia (18–9) and New Zealand (19–6). Now a year into the job it was time for Johnson to make his mark – and that test would come with the 2010 RBS 6 Nations.

So when England comprehensively outplayed Wales in their opening match at Twickenham, running in three tries in a 30–17 victory, it seemed as though a corner had finally been turned. It proved a false dawn. They struggled to a 17–12 victory over Italy in Rome, lost to Ireland (20–16) at Twickenham, drew with Scotland at Murrayfield (15–15) and rounded out a disappointing campaign with a 12–10 defeat against France in Paris. With a Rugby World Cup looming, it seemed as though England under Johnson had yet to find a way of winning the big matches.

All of which made their performances in the 2011 RBS 6 Nations all the more encouraging. England opened up with a 26–19 victory over Wales at the Millennium Stadium – their first in the Welsh capital since 2003, and went on to defeat Italy (59–13), France (17–9) and Scotland (22–16) at Twickenham. Victory over Ireland in Dublin would see them claim a first Grand Slam since 2003: they lost (24–8), but no one could argue against the fact that genuine progress had been made, and England travelled to the Rugby World Cup in New Zealand later in the year with quiet confidence.

England struggled from the start. They may have recorded comfortable, and expected, pool-round victories over Georgia (41–10) and Romania (67–3), the manner of their narrow victories over both Argentina (13–9) and Scotland (16–12) suggested all was not well within the England camp. And it came as little surprise when they fell to France (19–12) in the quarter-finals. The defeat prompted Johnson to call time on what had been an uneasy stint as England coach.

FOR THE RECORD

Born	9 March 1970, Solihull, West Midlands
Span as coach	1 July 2008–16 November 2011
Record as coach	Played – 38; Won – 21; Drew – 1; Lost – 16
Win % as coach	55%
Honours as coach	Six Nations (2011)

ENGLAND'S PERFORMANCE UNDER JOHNSON

Team	Mat	W	L	D	Win %	PF	PA	Diff
Argentina	4	3	1	0	75.00	88	57	+31
Australia	5	2	3	0	40.00	96	111	-15
France	4	2	2	0	50.00	73	50	+23
Georgia	1	1	0	0	100.00	41	10	+31
Ireland	4	1	3	0	25.00	57	67	-10
Italy	3	3	0	0	100.00	112	36	+76
New Zealand	3	0	3	0	0.00	28	77	-49
Pacific Islands	1	1	0	0	100.00	39	13	+26
Romania	1	1	0	0	100.00	67	3	+64
Samoa	1	1	0	0	100.00	26	13	+13
Scotland	4	3	0	1	87.50	79	55	+24
South Africa	2	0	2	0	0.00	17	63	-46
Wales	5	3	2	0	60.00	103	97	+6

STUART LANCASTER

Stuart Lancaster cut his coaching teeth first at Leeds Carnegie and then as the RFU's Elite Rugby Director (a role that tasked him with developing young English talent and running England's second-string Saxons team). And so when England found themselves looking for both a new coach and a new direction following their disappointing showing under Martin Johnson at the Rugby World Cup 2011, they had no hesitation in turning to the Cumbrian, albeit, initially at least, on a temporary basis.

Lancaster made his intentions clear from his opening game in charge against Scotland at Murrayfield, ringing the changes (ten of them from the side that had played against Scotland at the World Cup), handing the captaincy to Chris Robshaw (who, by that point, had a mere 53 minutes of Test match experience to his name) and calling up three players for their debuts. His bravery was rewarded when his new-look England side ran out 16–6 winners. They followed it up with a hard-fought 19–15 victory over Italy in a wintry Rome, before losing to Wales (who would go on to win the Grand Slam) 19–12 at Twickenham. Subsequent victories over France in Paris (24–22) and Ireland at Twickenham (30–9) brought down the curtain on what had been an encouraging campaign for England. The RFU certainly thought so, as Lancaster was handed the job on a permanent basis.

The rest of the year brought glimpses of what England could become under Lancaster, notably a draw against South Africa in Port Elizabeth and an easy 38–21 win against New Zealand at Twickenham (England's record victory over the All Blacks). And England's progress was confirmed with their performances in the 2013 RBS 6 Nations: they beat Scotland (38–18), Ireland (12–6), France (23–13) and Italy (18–11) to set up a title-deciding clash against Wales in Cardiff. England were overawed in the Millennium Stadium that day, losing 30–3, but the defeat, and the nature of it, would prove an important step on the journey for this England team: sometimes the best lessons learned are the hardest ones. England rounded out 2013 by recording a hat-trick of victories against Argentina and a 20–13 win against Australia at Twickenham – although they could not repeat their previous season's victory over the All Blacks, losing 30–22.

England
Rugby

If fans needed any proof that Lancaster had instilled character and belief in this England side, it came during the 2014 RBS 6 Nations. England overcame the intense disappointment of a last-gasp defeat to France in Paris (26–24) by beating Scotland (20–0), Ireland (13–10), Wales (29–18) and Italy (52–11) to finish second in the championship and claim a first Triple Crown since 2003. Later that summer, they gave the All Blacks an almighty scare in their own backyard too, running them close in two of the three Test matches. They stuttered in the 2014 QBE Autumn Internationals, losing to New Zealand and South Africa before beating Samoa and Australia. And when they beat Wales in Cardiff in the opening match of the 2015 RBS 6Nations, England fans started to believe they were about to witness something special. Ireland ended any dreams of a Grand Slam, however.

FOR THE RECORD

Born	9 October 1969, Penrith, Cumbria
Span as coach	8 December 2011–current
Record as coach	Played – 31; Won – 18; Drawn – 1; Lost – 12
Win % as coach	58%
Honours as coach	None

ENGLAND'S PERFORMANCE UNDER LANCASTER

Team	Mat	W	L	D	Win %	PF	PA	Diff
Argentina	3	3	0	0	100.00	114	41	+73
Australia	3	2	1	0	66.66	60	50	+10
Fiji	1	1	0	0	100.00	54	12	+42
France	4	3	1	0	75.00	126	96	+30
Ireland	4	3	1	0	75.00	64	44	+20
Italy	4	4	0	0	100.00	136	54	+82
New Zealand	6	1	5	0	16.66	136	159	-23
Samoa	1	1	0	0	100.00	28	9	+19
Scotland	4	4	0	0	100.00	96	37	+59
South Africa	5	0	4	1	10.00	101	119	-18
Wales	4	2	2	0	50.00	65	83	-18

**England
Rugby**

CHAPTER 6
ENGLAND FANTASY RUGBY TEAMS

It is the stuff of every rugby fan's dreams: take your favourite club team, wrack your brains to remember who had played for England while at the club, and then assemble an England XV from it. The following selections will no doubt prompt some debate, but here are a group of England XVs that could have made a serious impact on the pitch.

= Players marked with an asterisk also appeared in Test matches for the British Lions or British and Irish Lions.

BATH ENGLAND XV

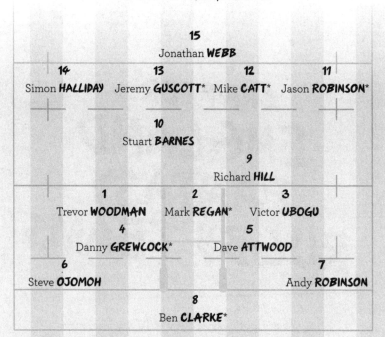

15
Jonathan **WEBB**

14
Simon **HALLIDAY**

13
Jeremy **GUSCOTT***

12
Mike **CATT***

11
Jason **ROBINSON***

10
Stuart **BARNES**

9
Richard **HILL**

1
Trevor **WOODMAN**

2
Mark **REGAN***

3
Victor **UBOGU**

4
Danny **GREWCOCK***

5
Dave **ATTWOOD**

6
Steve **OJOMOH**

7
Andy **ROBINSON**

8
Ben **CLARKE***

REPLACEMENTS
Matt **STEVENS**, Gareth **CHILCOTT**, Lee **MEARS***, Phil **DE GLANVILLE**,
Iain **BALSHAW***, Jon **CALLARD**

Did You Know That?
Established in 1865, Bath Rugby Club is one of the oldest and most prestigious clubs in world rugby. Herbert Fuller is generally recognized as being the club's first international: he won the first of six caps for England against Ireland at Lansdowne Road on 6 February 1882 – a match that ended in a 0–0 draw.

England Rugby

GLOUCESTER ENGLAND XV

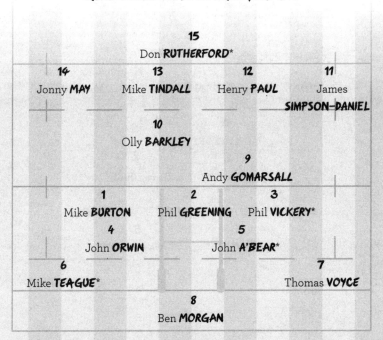

15
Don **RUTHERFORD***

14
Jonny **MAY**

13
Mike **TINDALL**

12
Henry **PAUL**

11
James **SIMPSON–DANIEL**

10
Olly **BARKLEY**

9
Andy **GOMARSALL**

1
Mike **BURTON**

2
Phil **GREENING**

3
Phil **VICKERY***

4
John **ORWIN**

5
John **A'BEAR***

6
Mike **TEAGUE***

7
Thomas **VOYCE**

8
Ben **MORGAN**

REPLACEMENTS
Phil **BLAKEWAY**, Trevor **WOODMAN**, Dave **SIMS**, James **FORRESTER**,
Freddie **BURNS**, Tom **VOYCE**

Did You Know That?
Lock forward John A'Bear was Gloucester's youngest-ever captain. He did not win a cap for England, but did tour Argentina with Great Britain in 1936. His best playing days surely lay ahead of him when the Second World War broke out in 1939, and he retired from the game in 1946 due to business commitments.

HARLEQUINS ENGLAND XV

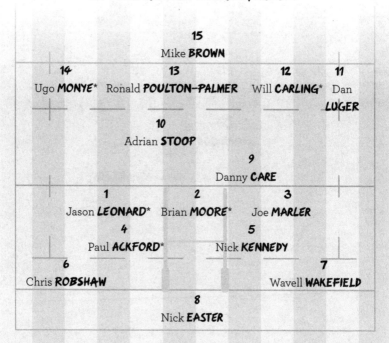

15
Mike **BROWN**

14
Ugo **MONYE***

13
Ronald **POULTON–PALMER**

12
Will **CARLING***

11
Dan **LUGER**

10
Adrian **STOOP**

9
Danny **CARE**

1
Jason **LEONARD***

2
Brian **MOORE***

3
Joe **MARLER**

4
Paul **ACKFORD***

5
Nick **KENNEDY**

6
Chris **ROBSHAW**

7
Wavell **WAKEFIELD**

8
Nick **EASTER**

REPLACEMENTS

Andy **MULLINS**, Mickey **SKINNER**, Tony **DIPROSE**, Andy **GOMARSALL**, Marland **YARDE**, Paul **SACKEY**

Did You Know That?

The origins of Harlequins Rugby Football Club lie with the Hampstead Football Club. When the latter club decided to change its name, presumably to broaden its geographic horizons, a majority of its members chose the name Harlequins. The choice led to a split in the club, however. Those who did not like the new name went on to form another club, known today as Wasps.

England Rugby

LEICESTER ENGLAND XV

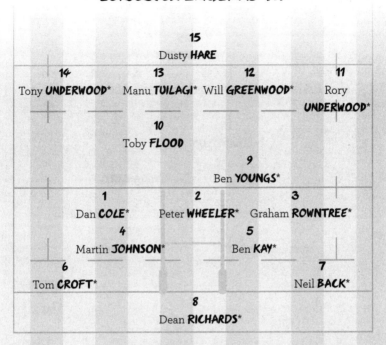

15
Dusty **HARE**

14
Tony **UNDERWOOD***

13
Manu **TUILAGI***

12
Will **GREENWOOD***

11
Rory **UNDERWOOD***

10
Toby **FLOOD**

9
Ben **YOUNGS***

1
Dan **COLE***

2
Peter **WHEELER***

3
Graham **ROWNTREE***

4
Martin **JOHNSON***

5
Ben **KAY***

6
Tom **CROFT***

7
Neil **BACK***

8
Dean **RICHARDS***

REPLACEMENTS

Julian **WHITE***, Tom **YOUNGS***, Geoff **PARLING***, Martin **CORRY***,
Austin **HEALEY***, Clive **WOODWARD***

Did You Know That?

Winger Jack Miles was Leicester Tigers' first international. He made his one and only appearance for England against Wales at Swansea on 10 January 1903 – a match England lost 21–5.

NORTHAMPTON ENGLAND XV

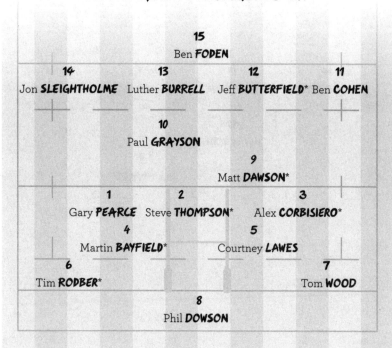

15
Ben **FODEN**

14
Jon **SLEIGHTHOLME**

13
Luther **BURRELL**

12
Jeff **BUTTERFIELD***

11
Ben **COHEN**

10
Paul **GRAYSON**

9
Matt **DAWSON***

1
Gary **PEARCE**

2
Steve **THOMPSON***

3
Alex **CORBISIERO***

4
Martin **BAYFIELD***

5
Courtney **LAWES**

6
Tim **RODBER***

7
Tom **WOOD**

8
Phil **DOWSON**

REPLACEMENTS
David **POWELL**, Don **WHITE**, Dylan **HARTLEY**, Peter **LARTER***,
Dickie **JEEPS***, Nick **BEAL**

Did You Know That?
Dickie Jeeps has played in more Test matches for the British Lions than any other England player in history. The scrum-half made 13 appearances for the Lions on three tours between 1955 and 1962 – only Ireland's Willie John McBride (17) has made more Test appearances for the legendary touring side.

England
Rugby

SALE ENGLAND XV

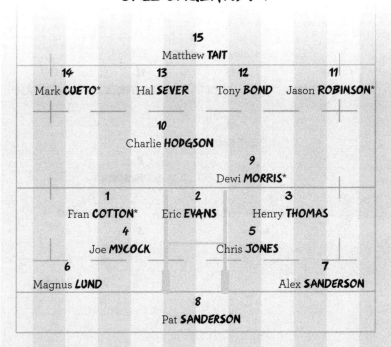

15
Matthew **TAIT**

14
Mark **CUETO***

13
Hal **SEVER**

12
Tony **BOND**

11
Jason **ROBINSON***

10
Charlie **HODGSON**

9
Dewi **MORRIS***

1
Fran **COTTON***

2
Eric **EVANS**

3
Henry **THOMAS**

4
Joe **MYCOCK**

5
Chris **JONES**

6
Magnus **LUND**

7
Alex **SANDERSON**

8
Pat **SANDERSON**

REPLACEMENTS
Stuart **TURNER**, Andy **TITTERRELL**, Steve **SMITH**, Barrie-Jon **MATHER**,
Steve **HANLEY**, David **REES**

Did You Know That?
Hal Sever made his debut for England against New Zealand at Twickenham in 1936. Another debutant, Prince Alexander Obolensky, may have stolen the headlines that day with his two-try performance, but Sever scored England's third try that day in a 13–0 victory – England's first-ever victory over the All Blacks.

SARACENS ENGLAND XV

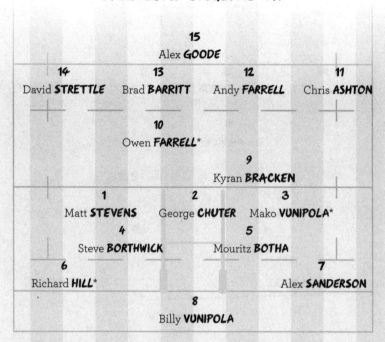

15
Alex **GOODE**

14
David **STRETTLE**

13
Brad **BARRITT**

12
Andy **FARRELL**

11
Chris **ASHTON**

10
Owen **FARRELL***

9
Kyran **BRACKEN**

1
Matt **STEVENS**

2
George **CHUTER**

3
Mako **VUNIPOLA***

4
Steve **BORTHWICK**

5
Mouritz **BOTHA**

6
Richard **HILL***

7
Alex **SANDERSON**

8
Billy **VUNIPOLA**

REPLACEMENTS
Julian **WHITE***, Matt **CAIRNS**, George **KRUIS**, Tony **DIPROSE**,
Charlie **HODGSON**, Richard **WIGGLESWORTH**

Did You Know That?
*Saracens Rugby Club was founded in 1876 by the Old Boys of the
Philological School in Marylebone, London (which later became
St Marylebone Grammar School). The club's name is said to have
come from the "endurance, enthusiasm and invincibility displayed
by Saladin's desert warriors", known as the Saracens, during the
12th-century Crusades.*

England
Rugby

WASPS ENGLAND XV

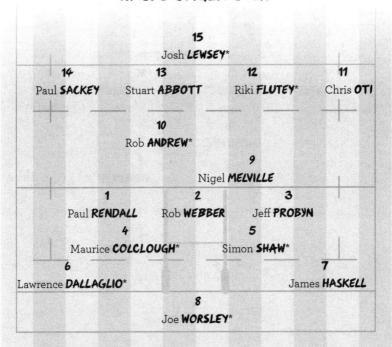

15
Josh **LEWSEY***

14
Paul **SACKEY**

13
Stuart **ABBOTT**

12
Riki **FLUTEY***

11
Chris **OTI**

10
Rob **ANDREW***

9
Nigel **MELVILLE**

1
Paul **RENDALL**

2
Rob **WEBBER**

3
Jeff **PROBYN**

4
Maurice **COLCLOUGH***

5
Simon **SHAW***

6
Lawrence **DALLAGLIO***

7
James **HASKELL**

8
Joe **WORSLEY***

REPLACEMENTS
Will **GREEN**, Matt **MULLAN**, Joe **LAUNCHBURY**, Tom **REES**,
Danny **CIPRIANI**, Christian **WADE**

Did You Know That?
*On 13 May 1989, three members of the Wasps club captained
England at different levels: Rob Andrew captained the senior team
against Romania; David Pegler captained the B team against
Spain; and Steve Pilgrim led the Under-21 side against Romania.
For the record, all three England teams won on the day.*

ARMED SERVICES ENGLAND XV

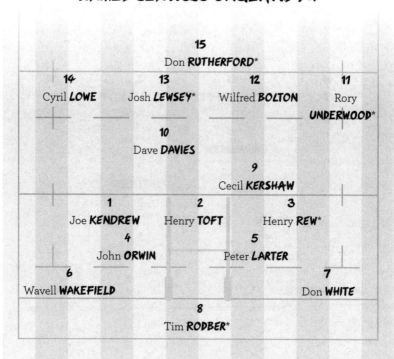

15
Don **RUTHERFORD***

14
Cyril **LOWE**

13
Josh **LEWSEY***

12
Wilfred **BOLTON**

11
Rory **UNDERWOOD***

10
Dave **DAVIES**

9
Cecil **KERSHAW**

1
Joe **KENDREW**

2
Henry **TOFT**

3
Henry **REW***

4
John **ORWIN**

5
Peter **LARTER**

6
Wavell **WAKEFIELD**

7
Don **WHITE**

8
Tim **RODBER***

REPLACEMENTS

Charles **SHERRARD**, Robert **HENDERSON**, Reg **HIGGINS***, Herbert **GODWIN**, Arthur **HARRISON**, Semesa **ROKODUGUNI**

Did You Know That?

There will always be an inextricable link between rugby and the Armed Forces. William Webb Ellis, the Rugby School pupil credited with inventing the game when he picked up the ball and ran with it during a game of football, was the son of an Army officer, James Ellis.

OXBRIDGE ENGLAND XV

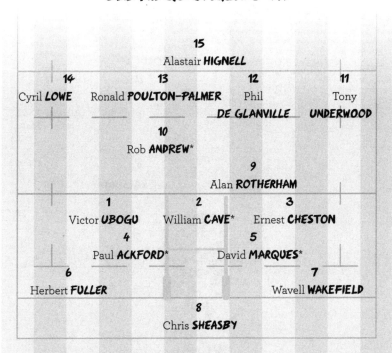

15
Alastair **HIGNELL**

14
Cyril **LOWE**

13
Ronald **POULTON-PALMER**

12
Phil
DE GLANVILLE

11
Tony
UNDERWOOD

10
Rob **ANDREW***

9
Alan **ROTHERHAM**

1
Victor **UBOGU**

2
William **CAVE***

3
Ernest **CHESTON**

4
Paul **ACKFORD***

5
David **MARQUES***

6
Herbert **FULLER**

7
Wavell **WAKEFIELD**

8
Chris **SHEASBY**

REPLACEMENTS

Robert **WILLIAM-BELL**, Simon **HALLIDAY**, Damian **HOPLEY**, Stuart **BARNES**,
Alexander **OBOLENSKY**, Marcus **ROSE**

Did You Know That?

*Rugby, or at least an early version of the game, is said to have
arrived at Cambridge University in 1836, when former Rugby School
pupil Albert Pell arrived at Trinity College. Oxford University
Rugby Club was formed in 1869.*

England
Rugby

CHAPTER 7
ENGLAND
RUGBY QUOTES

Rugby followers today are used to opinion;
they are bombarded with it from every
angle – the radio, television, Internet, and
in the newspapers. And although you don't
have to look too hard to find reports on
some of England's greatest achievements,
the descriptions of these milestones are
more than often provided by journalists. The
following pages contain some memorable
quotes from England players about some of
the best days – and a few of the worst – in
English rugby history, as they saw it through
their eyes.

1913 GRAND SLAM

"Poulton-Palmer was a centre threequarter of the highest type, having a deceptive swerve and sound in defence. He was exceedingly popular with a host of friends and admirers."

Leonard Tosswill *on Ronald Poulton-Palmer*

"The English forwards were superior to their opponents in every game, and, time after time, an opportune dribble produced a 50-yard advance and prevented a probable adverse score."

Ronald Poulton-Palmer *commenting on England's 1913 Grand Slam-winning pack.*

1914 GRAND SLAM

"I have often been asked my opinion as to the comparative playing strength of the [1921 and 1923 Grand Slam] teams compared with the 1914 team. An answer, which is accurate and without qualification, is hard to find. If the personal element could be eliminated and rugby football theories treated dogmatically and logically, then perhaps one might conclude the 1914 team was better."

England fly-half **Dave Davies**, *when asked which was better – the 1914, the 1921 or the 1923 England Grand Slam-winning team.*

"I shall never play at Twickenham again."

The last reported words of **Ronald Poulton-Palmer** *before his death from a sniper's bullet in 1915.*

1921 GRAND SLAM

"Before the Scotch match [at Inverleith in 1921], Scotsmen (my Scotch friends tell me) had always regarded English forwards as soft. This time, the English pack was definitely the better of the two. After the game, one of the Scotch forwards, ruefully rubbing his shin, complained to me that we had used the boot too much. I told him Scotland had set the example in the past."

Wavell Wakefield reflects on the efforts of England's pack during their match against Scotland at Inverleith in 1921. An 18-0 victory set up a chance for a Grand Slam against France – a match England would go on to win 10-6.

1923 GRAND SLAM

"The [final] game [of the 1923 Five Nations] played in France was no easy obstacle [but] proved successful. It was unfortunate for England that Lowe and Smallwood were both crocked in the first ten minutes of the game. As on other occasions earlier in the season, England owed her victory mainly to the skill of the forwards."

*England captain **Dave Davies** reflects on England's 12-3 Grand Slam-clinching victory over France in the 1923 Five Nations.*

"He was a very great player and a most inspiring captain, and he has certainly had a deep and lasting influence on the game."

Wavell Wakefield on England's 1923 Grand Slam-winning captain Dave Davies, who retired from international rugby following the 1923 campaign.

1924 GRAND SLAM

"Never was there a side – no, not even a club side – that combined
so perfectly as did Davies' last England side of 1923, or
Wakefield's first of 1924. In both these sides you had an ideal
mixture of individualism and combination."

Dai Gent, *who played five Tests for England between 1905 and 1910*

"Considering the famous players who had dropped out of the side,
I think 1924 must be regarded as a most satisfactory season, and,
save in 1921, I cannot remember ever playing in a better pack."

Wavell Wakefield *reflects on England's 1924 Grand Slam-winning
campaign.*

"There was nothing particularly memorable about the French
match at Twickenham [in 1924]. It was in that game there was
a sudden upheaval in the scrum and Reg Edwards emerged
and let fly at an opposing forward, not without reason, for when
the referee went over to find out what it was all about, Edwards
simply pointed to his cheek, where the Frenchman's teeth marks
were plainly visible.
 Our backs supported us very well and our forwards at that time
fitted in with one another excellently, so that we were able to win
by a record margin [of 19–0 against Scotland], though I must say
everything went right with us and no mistakes were made with
our kicks at goal."

According to **Wavell Wakefield**, *England had to overcome
France's uncompromising tactics during their 19–7 victory at
Twickenham before going on to beat Scotland 19–0 in their final
match to claim a fifth Grand Slam.*

"In any classification of forwards, W.W. Wakefield must be placed very near the top. Possessed of all the physical qualities necessary for the highest standard, he obtained, very early, by assiduous practice and thorough training, a pre-eminent position in the rugby football world."

England's 1923 Grand Slam-winning captain **Dave Davies** *examines the qualities that made Wavell Wakefield one of the game's all-time greats.*

1928 GRAND SLAM

"Mention ought to be made of the success of R. Cove-Smith's side in 1928 ... But it was the poor quality of international football generally, together with Cove-Smith's effective handling of his side, that gave England her victories, rather than the brilliance of her play."

Dai Gent *on England's 1928 Grand Slam-winning team.*

1957 GRAND SLAM

"Here was a return to those basic principles which many doubters had feared were on the wane. The orderly, inexorable wearing down of the opposition by a well-balanced, splendidly equipped pack of forwards, and the consequent smoothing of the passage of the ball through the half-backs to an alert and offensive three-quarter line imbued incessantly with the idea of attack. Scotland, to their eternal credit, were infected with the same outlook."

The Times *article following England's 1957 Grand Slam-clinching victory over Scotland.*

"C.R. Jacobs and G.W. Hastings helped to form the best front row that England have had since the war."

The Times *was in little doubt as to where the credit should lie for England's 1957 Grand Slam-winning campaign.*

1980 GRAND SLAM

"I chased a Paul Dodge kick and caught it, leaving me 60 yards to sprint for the line. I was thinking, 'This is our day, here I am just about to score my third try in a Grand Slam game.'"

*England wing **John Carleton**, who scored three tries (the first England hat-trick since 1924) during England's Grand Slam-clinching victory over Scotland in 1980 – the country's first for 23 years.*

"Billy [Beaumont] was a great guy – a real top. That whole England team was a bunch of characters, everyone was a character and he held it together. Billy was great for us, the management and the supporters – the perfect captain."

***John Scott**, England's No.8 during the 1980 Grand Slam campaign, on captain Bill Beaumont.*

"It was a feat that meant a lot to us. We knew we had achieved something but I believe it meant a lot more to the likes of Billy [Beaumont], Fran [Cotton], Nearo [Tony Neary] and Roger [Uttley] – outstanding players who had not won anything with England, who had failed and failed a lot before."

*Former England centre **Paul Dodge** on what the 1980 Grand Slam meant to the team.*

RUGBY WORLD CUP 1987

"The quarter-final against Wales in 1987 – along with the third-place playoff game in 1995 – were the worst two games I ever played in, and I pity anybody who had to watch them. Awful … It was a dreadful game and we played very badly."

Brian Moore *on England's quarter-final defeat to Wales at the Rugby World Cup 1987.*

"The inaugural World Cup was a very exciting prospect, but we approached it with no professionalism at all. The attitude was that it might be the first and last World Cup. Everyone was incredibly sceptical. We had a hell of a party anyway.

Dean Richards *reveals that England's mindset might not have been spot-on at the Rugby World Cup 1987.*

1991 GRAND SLAM

"Come 1991 and we were in business-like mode. [In 1990] we had let a Grand Slam go begging through arrogance and that wasn't going to happen again. We were going to seal the deal this year; grind out that elusive Grand Slam."

Will Carling *speaks of England's determination to win the Grand Slam in 1991.*

"I think everyone on that English team would say that the fear of losing we all had was far greater than the joy we got from winning. I think a lot of great teams have that."

Jeremy Guscott *on the sense of relief that pervaded the England camp after winning the Grand Slam in 1991.*

1992 GRAND SLAM

"By 1992 we were a complete team. We could be steely and tight, but also expansive and free-scoring. We had learned how to always take our chances, and we were in the groove."

Rory Underwood *on England's 1992 Grand Slam-winning team.*

"We were good, very good, at the height of our powers, and we won the Grand Slam with plenty to spare, which is rare."

Will Carling *on England's Grand Slam in 1992.*

1995 GRAND SLAM

"It was an indication of how much English rugby had improved that we were made heavy favourites to achieve the feat [of winning a Grand Slam]."

Brian Moore *on England's 1995 Grand Slam.*

RUGBY WORLD CUP 1995

"He's a freak, and the sooner he goes away the better."

*England captain **Will Carling** on Jonah Lomu after the giant New Zealand wing had left England's Rugby World Cup 1995 dreams in tatters.*

"I don't know about us not having a Plan B when things went wrong; we looked like we didn't have a Plan A either."

*Former England coach **Geoff Cooke** after England's semi-final defeat to New Zealand at Rugby World Cup 1995.*

RUGBY WORLD CUP 1999

"They've done everything they possibly could to do something special and it's not happened."

England coach **Clive Woodward** *after England were beaten 44–21 by South Africa in the Rugby World Cup quarter-finals.*

2003 GRAND SLAM

"I can't say how good these guys are. They are the toughest guys I have ever worked with, physically and mentally. I was confident we were going to win, if we held on to the ball. Ireland are a good team, but I am delighted with the outcome. The players deserve this, big time. I'm lucky to be leading them."

England coach **Clive Woodward** *after England beat Ireland to win the Grand Slam in 2003.*

"We have had our disappointments over the years. It's a credit to our players and coaches. But we have finally got it."

England captain **Martin Johnson** *savours Grand Slam success in 2003.*

"It's just what this squad deserves, and it will stand to us in what will be a massive year. Winning the Grand Slam is the perfect platform for us. You are judged on the games you win, and up until Sunday we had not won much to be honest."

England No.8 **Lawrence Dallaglio** *on the importance of winning a Grand Slam in 2003 with a Rugby World Cup coming up later in the year.*

RUGBY WORLD CUP 2003

"I can't say enough about the team, because we had the lead and we lost it, but we came back. And I can't say enough about Wilko at the end. You've got to give credit to Australia, they're a very good team and they made it very difficult for us."

Martin Johnson after becoming the first England captain to lead his side to Rugby World Cup victory.

"There is a lot of pressure on him and he gets built up to a degree where people expect superhuman stuff from him and most of the stuff he does is verging on that. To call him a kicker doesn't do him justice because the work he puts in on the field and in all aspects of his game is fantastic. He is a very special player."

*More from **Martin Johnson**, this time on Jonny Wilkinson.*

"I feel like a very proud member of a very proud team. This is not the end of our journey, it's part of the road we're on and we have to use it to motivate us further. I did have a couple of beers, but that was only really as a solidarity thing with the other guys. There are times for letting yourself go, but Saturday night I just wanted to let it all soak in."

*England's Rugby World Cup final hero **Jonny Wilkinson.***

"We came very close to blowing it. Every decision seemed to go against them, and yet they still won, and that is the sign of a champion team. They are a great bunch of players with a great captain, and I am just very proud and privileged to be in charge of them."

Clive Woodward

"It might be difficult to understand, but I never felt we were going to lose that game – it was the inner steel, the inner belief within the squad that whatever it takes we will win."

Lawrence Dallaglio

"To say we celebrated in style would be the understatement of the year. We've had a big one – an absolute blinder and I think it's been richly deserved."

Matt Dawson *confirms that England celebrated their Rugby World Cup success in style.*

RUGBY WORLD CUP 2007

"They did fantastically well getting into the final, but in days to come, they'll reflect on what they've done and be really proud. I thought they rose to the occasion absolutely magnificently."

England coach **Brian Ashton** *after watching his team lose to South Africa in the final.*

"We've had a magical time. Fair play to South Africa. They were the better team and this is their victory. We have to wait for four years so they better enjoy it."

England's Rugby World Cup 2007 captain **Phil Vickery.**

"It's disappointing. We gave it everything. At times we got close enough and we never really felt we were going to lose. We had a lot of ground to catch up in this tournament and the guys all took the responsibility. I was proud of them all. It has been a hell of a journey."

Jonny Wilkinson

England
Rugby

CHAPTER 8
ENGLAND RUGBY SONGS

There can be few greater sounds in world sport than the Twickenham crowd in full voice, driving their team forward with a hearty rendition of "Swing Low, Sweet Chariot". But that is not the only song associated with the England rugby team. The songs featured in the following pages will ensure that you keep up with the most vocal supporters on match day – and, what's more, you'll know all the words.

SWING LOW SWEET CHARIOT

Chorus

Swing low, sweet chariot

Coming for to carry me home,
Swing low, sweet chariot,
Coming for to carry me home.

I looked over Jordan, and what did I see

Coming for to carry me home?
A band of angels coming after me,
Coming for to carry me home.

Chorus

Sometimes I'm up, and sometimes I'm down,
(Coming for to carry me home),
But still my soul feels heavenly bound.
(Coming for to carry me home).

Chorus

The brightest day that I can say,
(Coming for to carry me home).
When Jesus washed my sins away,
(Coming for to carry me home).

Chorus

If you get there before I do,
(Coming for to carry me home).
Tell all my friends I'm coming there too.
(Coming for to carry me home).

Chorus

LAND OF HOPE AND GLORY

Dear Land of Hope, thy hope is crowned,
God make thee mightier yet!
On Sov'ran brows, beloved, renowned,
Once more thy crown is set.
Thine equal laws, by Freedom gained,
Have ruled thee well and long;
By Freedom gained, by Truth maintained,
Thine Empire shall be strong.

Chorus

Land of Hope and Glory, Mother of the Free,
How shall we extol thee, who are born of thee?
Wider still and wider shall thy bounds be set;
God, who made thee mighty, make thee mightier yet,
God, who made thee mighty, make thee mightier yet.

Thy fame is ancient as the days,
As Ocean large and wide:
A pride that dares, and heeds not praise,
A stern and silent pride;
Not that false joy that dreams content

With what our sires have won;
The blood a hero sire hath spent

Still nerves a hero son.

Chorus

GOD SAVE THE QUEEN

God save our gracious Queen!
Long live our noble Queen!
God save the Queen!
Send her victorious,
Happy and glorious,
Long to reign over us,
God save the Queen.

[unused second verse]

Thy choicest gifts in store
On her be pleased to pour,
Long may she reign.
May she defend our laws,
And ever give us cause,
To sing with heart and voice,
God save the Queen.

ABIDE WITH ME

Abide with me; fast falls the eventide;
The darkness deepens; Lord, with me abide;
When other helpers fail and comforts flee,
Help of the helpless, oh, abide with me.

Swift to its close ebbs out life's little day;
Earth's joys grow dim, its glories pass away;
Change and decay in all around I see –

O Thou who changest not, abide with me.

I need Thy presence every passing hour;
What but Thy grace can foil the tempter's pow'r?
Who, like Thyself, my guide and stay can be?
Through cloud and sunshine, Lord, abide with me.

I fear no foe, with Thee at hand to bless;
Ills have no weight, and tears no bitterness;
Where is death's sting? Where, grave, thy victory?
I triumph still, if Thou abide with me.
Hold Thou Thy cross before my closing eyes;
Shine through the gloom and point me to the skies;
Heav'n's morning breaks, and earth's vain shadows flee;
In life, in death, O Lord, abide with me.

RULE BRITANNIA

When Britain first, at Heaven's command
Arose from out the azure main;
This was the charter of the land,
And guardian angels sang this strain:
Rule, Britannia! rule the waves:
"Britons never will be slaves."

The nations, not so blest as thee,
Must, in their turns, to tyrants fall;
While thou shalt flourish great and free,
The dread and envy of them all.
Rule, Britannia! rule the waves:
"Britons never will be slaves."

Still more majestic shalt thou rise,
More dreadful, from each foreign stroke;
As the loud blast that tears the skies,
Serves but to root thy native oak.
Rule, Britannia! rule the waves:
"Britons never will be slaves."

Thee haughty tyrants ne'er shall tame:
All their attempts to bend thee down,
Will but arouse thy generous flame;
But work their woe, and thy renown.
Rule, Britannia! rule the waves:
"Britons never will be slaves."

To thee belongs the rural reign;
Thy cities shall with commerce shine:
All thine shall be the subject main,
And every shore it circles thine.
Rule, Britannia! rule the waves:
"Britons never will be slaves."

The Muses, still with freedom found,

Shall to thy happy coast repair;
Blest Isle! With matchless beauty crown'd,
And manly hearts to guard the fair.
Rule, Britannia! rule the waves:
"Britons never will be slaves."

JERUSALEM

And did those feet in ancient time
Walk upon England's mountains green:
And was the holy Lamb of God,
On England's pleasant pastures seen!
And did the Countenance Divine,
Shine forth upon our clouded hills?
And was Jerusalem builded here,
Among these dark Satanic Mills?

Bring me my Bow of burning gold;
Bring me my Arrows of desire:
Bring me my Spear: O clouds unfold!
Bring me my Chariot of fire!
I will not cease from Mental Fight,
Nor shall my Sword sleep in my hand:
Till we have built Jerusalem,
In England's green and pleasant Land.

England
Rugby

CHAPTER 9
ENGLAND RUGBY QUIZZES

How well do you know the England Rugby team and the nation's famous history? In the previous chapters, all the great players, coaches and matches have been discussed. All the answers to the questions on the next few pages can be found earlier in this book, but how many of them can you get correctly without taking a peek?

QUIZ 1: ENGLAND FIRSTS

1 Who is credited with scoring England's first international try?

2 Who was England's first captain?

3 Who were the first team England recorded back-to-back victories over?

4 Who were England's first opponents under the new points-scoring system (i.e. when games were decided by points rather than by goals)?

5 Who was the first England player to score two tries in a match?

6 Who was the first England player to score three tries in a match?

7 Who was the first England player to score four tries in a match?

8 Who was the first England player to score a try at Twickenham?

9 Who was the first England player to kick a drop-goal?

10 Who was the first England player to play in ten internationals?

11 Who was the first England player to play in 20 internationals?

12 Who was the first England player to play in 50 internationals?

13 Who was the first player to captain England on ten occasions?

14 Who was the first player to score ten tries for England?

15 Who was the first player to score 20 tries for England?

16 Who were England's first opponents in the professional era?

17 Who was England's first coach?

18 Who was the first England coach to record ten victories?

19 Who was the first England player to score 100 points?

20 Who was the first England player to score 200 points?

QUIZ 2: ENGLAND IN THE HOME/ FIVE NATIONS (1883–1999)

1   When did England win the title for the first time?
2   Against which country did England record the most victories?
3   Against which country did England record the fewest victories?
4   What was England's biggest victory in the competition?
5   What was England's heaviest defeat in the competition?
6   Where did England play their first-ever home match in the competition?
7   At which venue did England record the most away victories?
8   Which England player made the most appearances?
9   Which England players scored the most points?
10 Which England player holds the record for the most points in a single match?
11 Which England player made the most appearances as captain?
12 Which England player holds the record for appearing on the winning side the most times?
13 Which England players hold the record for appearing on the losing side the most times?
14 Which England player holds the record for the most points on his Home Nations debut?
15 Who is credited with scoring England's first-ever try in a Home Nations match?
16 Which England players scored the most tries in the competition?
17 Which England player holds the record for scoring the most tries on his debut in the competition?
18 Which England player appeared in ten or more Home/Five Nations matches and was on the winning side every time?
19 Which England player holds the record for the most penalties kicked in the competition?
20 Which England player holds the record for the most drop-goals kicked in the competition?

QUIZ 3: ENGLAND IN THE SIX NATIONS (2000-)

1. Against which country have England recorded the most victories?
2. Against which country have England suffered the most defeats?
3. What is England's biggest victory in the Six Nations?
4. What is England's heaviest defeat in the Six Nations?
5. Against which country did England record their only draw in the Six Nations?
6. At which away ground have England enjoyed the most success in Six Nations matches?
7. What is England's biggest victory in an away match in the Six Nations?
8. Against which country have England conceded the most points in Six Nations matches?
9. What is the highest number of tries England have scored in a single Six Nations tournament?
10. What is the fewest number of tries England have scored in a single Six Nations tournament?
11. England have only recorded one Grand Slam in the Six Nations, in 2003. Who did they beat in the final round of matches to secure it?
12. Who is England's leading points-scorer in Six Nations matches?
13. Who is England's leading try-scorer in Six Nations matches?
14. Which England player holds the record for the most points scored in a single Six Nations match?
15. Which England player holds the record for the most tries scored in a single Six Nations match?
16. Who holds the record for the most points scored against England in Six Nations matches?
17. Which players share the record for the most tries scored against England in Six Nations matches?
18. Who holds the record for the most matches as England captain in Six Nations matches?
19. Which England player has made the most appearances in Six Nations matches?
20. Which England player holds the record for most appearances on a winning side in Six Nations matches?

QUIZ 4: ENGLAND AT THE RUGBY WORLD CUP

1   Who were England's first opponents at the Rugby World Cup?
2   Against whom did England record their first victory at the Rugby World Cup?
3   Who scored England's first Rugby World Cup try?
4   What is England's biggest Rugby World Cup victory?
5   What is England's heaviest Rugby World Cup defeat?
6   Against which two countries have England played the most Rugby World Cup matches?
7   Of the 16 countries England have played at the Rugby World Cup, who are the only team they have never beaten in the tournament?
8   Against which team have England scored the most points in Rugby World Cup matches?
9   Against which team have England scored the fewest points in Rugby World Cup matches?
10 Against which team have England scored the most tries in Rugby World Cup matches?
11 Who has made the most appearances at the Rugby World Cup for England?
12 Which England players share the record for the most starts in Rugby World Cup matches?
13 Which England player has scored the most points in Rugby World Cup matches?
14 Which England player has scored the most tries in Rugby World Cup matches?
15 Who is the only England player to score a try in a Rugby World Cup final?
16 Who holds the record for the most tries in a single Rugby World Cup match by an England player?
17 Who holds the record for the most points in a single Rugby World Cup match by an England player?
18 Who was the first England player to receive a yellow card in a Rugby World Cup match?
19 Who holds the record for the most points scored in a single match by an England captain at the Rugby World Cup?
20 Which two players hold the record for the most matches as England captain at the Rugby World Cup?

QUIZ 5: ENGLAND CHAMPIONS OF THE WORLD

1   Who scored England's first try in their opening match against Georgia at the Rugby World Cup 2003?

2   Who replaced Jonny Wilkinson at fly-half in that game?

3   Which two England players bagged two tries each in that game?

4   Who was England's only try-scorer in their 25–6 victory over South Africa at the Rugby World Cup 2003?

5   Name England's three try-scorers in their 35–22 victory over Samoa at the Rugby World Cup 2003.

6   In the absence of Martin Johnson, who captained England during their 111–13 victory over Uruguay at the Rugby World Cup 2003?

7   How many England players scored tries in that match?

8   Who was England's only try-scorer in their 28–17 quarter-final victory over Wales at the Rugby World Cup 2003?

9   How many drop-goals did Jonny Wilkinson score in England's 24–7 semi-final victory over France at the Rugby World Cup 2003?

10 Who was England's try-scorer in the Rugby World Cup 2003 final?

11 Who were the three unused replacements in the final?

12 Who was the only player to play in every minute of every England game at the Rugby World Cup 2003?

13 Who were England's leading try-scorers at Rugby World Cup 2003?

14 Which two England players made the most appearances as replacements at Rugby World Cup 2003?

15 Six players appeared in every game (although not every minute of every game) at Rugby World Cup 2003. Who were they?

16 Name the two England players who made only one appearance at the Rugby World Cup 2003.

17 Who was the oldest member of England's Rugby World Cup 2003 squad?

18 Who was the youngest member of England's Rugby World Cup 2003 squad?

19 Who was the only overseas-based player in England's Rugby World Cup 2003 squad?

20 Who handed the Webb Ellis trophy to Martin Johnson?

QUIZ 6: ENGLAND AT TWICKENHAM

1 Who were England's first-ever opponents at Twickenham?
2 Over which country have England recorded the most victories at Twickenham?
3 Against which country have England lost the most matches at Twickenham?
4 What is England's biggest victory at Twickenham?
5 What is England's heaviest defeat at Twickenham?
6 Which England player scored the first-ever try at Twickenham?
7 Which England player has scored the most tries at Twickenham?
8 Which non-England player has scored the most tries at Twickenham?
9 Which England player holds the record for scoring the most tries in a single match at Twickenham?
10 Which England player holds the record for scoring the most points at Twickenham?
11 Which non-England player holds the record for scoring the most points at Twickenham?
12 Which England player holds the record for scoring the most points in a single match at Twickenham?
13 Which non-England player holds the record for scoring the most points in a single match at Twickenham?
14 Who was the first player to receive a yellow card at Twickenham?
15 Who was the first England player to receive a yellow card at Twickenham?
16 Who was the first player to be sent off at Twickenham?
17 Who is the only England player to be sent off at Twickenham?
18 Which England player has made the most appearances at Twickenham?
19 Which non-England player has made the most appearances at Twickenham?
20 Which England player holds the record for being on the losing side the most times at Twickenham?

QUIZ 7: ENGLAND RECORDS

1 Who is England's youngest-ever player?
2 Who is England's oldest-ever player?
3 Who is England's most-capped player?
4 Who was England's most-capped player in the amateur era?
5 Who was England's longest-serving player?
6 Who holds the record for the most consecutive Test appearances for England?
7 Who is England's all-time leading points-scorer?
8 Who holds the England record for the most points scored in a single match?
9 Who was England's leading points-scorer in the amateur era?
10 Who was England's longest-serving captain solely in the amateur era?
11 Who is England's all-time leading try-scorer?
12 Which three England players hold the record for scoring the most tries (five) in a single match?
13 Who was the first England player to score three tries in a single Rugby World Cup match?
14 Name the two other England players to score three tries or more in a single Rugby World Cup match.
15 Who holds the record for the most tries scored by an England player at a single Rugby World Cup tournament?
16 Who holds the record for the most tries scored by an England player in a single Home/Five/Six Nations tournament?
17 What is England's longest winning sequence?
18 England's record points haul in a single Home/Five/Six Nations Championship is 229. In what year did they achieve the feat?
19 What is England's longest winning sequence in the Home/Five/Six Nations Championship?
20 What is England's longest winning sequence at the Rugby World Cup?

QUIZ 8: ENGLAND CAPTAINS

1   Which player holds the record for the most appearances as England captain?

2   Who was the first player to captain England on ten occasions?

3   Of the 46 players to captain England on five or more occasions, who has the worst winning percentage?

4   Who has scored the most points as England captain?

5   Who has scored the most tries as England captain?

6   Which two players share the record for suffering the most defeats as England captain?

7   Who was the first England captain to lead his side to a Grand Slam?

8   Only four players have captained England on debut. Who are they?

9   Which two players share the record for the most points scored in a single match as England captain?

10 Which player holds the record for the most tries scored in a single match by an England captain?

11 Will Carling holds the record for the most wins as England captain against a single opponent (eight). Who is the opponent?

12 Chris Robshaw holds the record for the most defeats as England captain against a single opponent. Who is the opponent?

13 Who was the first player to captain England on five occasions?

14 Who was the first England player to captain England on 20 occasions?

15 Which player holds the record for captaining England in the most drawn matches?

16 Which England captains have the best winning percentage at the Rugby World Cup?

17 Which England captain has the worst winning percentage at the Rugby World Cup?

18 Which two England captains hold the record for the most victories in Rugby World Cup matches?

19 Which England captain has scored the most points in Rugby World Cup matches?

20 Who was England's oldest captain?

QUIZ 9: ENGLAND AGAINST SOUTH AFRICA, NEW ZEALAND AND AUSTRALIA (SANZAR)

1   When did England record their first victory over South Africa?
2   When did England record their first victory over Australia?
3   When did England record their first victory over New Zealand?
4   When did England record their first away victory over South Africa?
5   When did England record their first away victory over Australia?
6   When did England record their first away victory over New Zealand?
7   Against which of the SANZAR countries do England have the best record?
8   Against which of the SANZAR countries do England have the worst record?
9   What is England's biggest victory over South Africa?
10 What is England's heaviest defeat against South Africa?
11 What is England's biggest victory over Australia?
12 What is England's heaviest defeat against Australia?
13 What is England's biggest victory over New Zealand?
14 What is England's heaviest defeat against New Zealand?
15 Which England player holds the record for the most points scored against the SANZAR countries?
16 Who is the only England player apart from Jonny Wilkinson to have scored more than 100 points against the SANZAR countries?
17 Which England player holds the record for the most tries scored against the SANZAR countries?
18 Which England players hold the record for the most points scored in a single match against the SANZAR countries?
19 Which England players hold the record for the most tries scored in a single match against the SANZAR countries?
20 Which England player has made the most appearances against the SANZAR countries?

QUIZ 10: ENGLAND AWAY

1   Against which country have England recorded the most away victories?

2   Against which country did England record their first away victory?

3   Who were England's opponents in their first away match in the southern hemisphere?

4   Against which country have England recorded the fewest away victories?

5   Against which country have England suffered the most away defeats?

6   Against whom have England scored the most points in away matches?

7   Against whom have England scored the most tries in away matches?

8   What is England's biggest away victory?

9   What is England's heaviest away defeat?

10 Which player holds the England record for the most appearances in away matches?

11 Which England player has scored the most tries in matches away from home?

12 Which England player has scored the most points in away matches?

13 Apart from Jonny Wilkinson, five other England players have scored more than 100 points in away matches. Who are they?

14 Which England player holds the record for the most points scored in a single away match?

15 Which England players hold the record for the most tries scored in a single away match?

16 Who was the first England player to score three tries in a single away match?

17 What are the most points England have scored in an away match they have gone on to lose?

18 Who has captained England in the most away matches?

19 Who was the first England player to be sent off in an away match?

20 Name the two other England players to receive their marching orders in an away match?

England
Rugby

ANSWERS

QUIZ 1: ENGLAND FIRSTS

1 Reginald Birkett, v Scotland, 1871; **2** Frederic Stokes; **3** Ireland (Feb 1875 and Dec 1875); **4** New Zealand Natives, Blackheath, 16 Feb 1889; **5** William Hutchinson (v Ireland, The Oval, 5 Feb 1887); **6** Henry Taylor (v Ireland, Manchester, 5 Feb 1881); **7** George Burton (v Wales, Blackheath, 19 Feb 1881); **8** Fred Chapman (v Wales, 15 Jan 1910); **9** Harold Freeman (v Scotland, The Oval, 5 Feb 1872); **10** Lennard Stokes (12 matches, 1875–81); **11** John Birkett (21 matches, 1906–12); **12** Peter Winterbottom (58 matches, 1982–93); **13** Dave Davies (11 matches as captain between 1921 and 1923); **14** John Birkett (10 tries, 1906–12); **15** Rory Underwood (49 tries, 1984–96); **16** South Africa (Twickenham, 18 Nov 1995 – they lost 24–14); **17** Don White, appointed in 1969; **18** Mike Davis (10 wins between 1979 and 1982); **19** Bob Hiller (138 points, 1968–72); **20** Dusty Hare (240 points, 1974–84).

QUIZ 2: ENGLAND IN THE HOME/FIVE NATIONS (1883–1999)

1 1883; **2** Ireland (58 wins in 103 matches); **3** France (36 wins in 70 matches); **4** 46–6 v Ireland, Lansdowne Road, 15 Feb 1997; **5** 6–33 v Scotland, Murrayfield, 15 Feb 1986; **6** Whalley Range, Manchester (v Ireland, 5 Feb 1893); **7** Lansdowne Road, Dublin (24 wins in 50 matches); **8** Rory Underwood (30 matches); **9** Rob Andrew and Paul Grayson (185 points); **10** Rob Andrew (24 points v Scotland, Twickenham, 18 Mar 1995); **11** Will Carling (32 matches); **12** Rory Underwood (32 matches); **13** David Duckham, Tony Neary, John Pullin and Peter Wheeler (20 matches); **14** Grahame Parker (15 points v Ireland, Lansdowne Road, 12 Feb 1938); **15** Wilfred Bolton (v Wales, Swansea, 16 Dec 1882); **16** Cyril Lowe and Rory Underwood (18 tries); **17** Danny Lambert (five tries v France, Richmond, 5 Jan 1907); **18** Dave Davies (15 wins in 15 matches between 1913 and 1923); **19** Dusty Hare (50); **20** Rob Andrew (nine).

QUIZ 3: ENGLAND IN THE SIX NATIONS (2000–)

1 Italy (played 16, won 16); **2** Ireland (9 defeats); **3** 80–23 v Italy, Twickenham, 17 Feb 2001; **4** 13–43 v Ireland, Croke Park, Dublin, 24 Feb 2007; **5** Scotland (15–15, Murrayfield, 13 Mar 2010); **6** Stadio Flaminio, Rome (six wins in six matches); **7** 59–12 v Italy, Rome, 18 Mar 2000; **8** France (296 points in 16 matches); **9** 29 (in 2001); **10** 5 (in 2013); **11** Ireland (42–6 in Dublin – *Ireland were also playing for the Grand Slam*; **12** Jonny Wilkinson (486 points); **13** Ben Cohen (16 tries); **14** Jonny Wilkinson (35 points v Italy, Twickenham, 17 Feb 2001); **15** Chris Ashton (4 v Italy, Twickenham, 12 Feb 2011); **16** Ronan O'Gara (Ireland – 92 points); **17** Mirco Bergamasco (Italy), Tommy Bowe, Shane Horgan and Brian O'Driscoll (all Ireland) – four; **18** Chris Robshaw (20 matches); **19** Joe Worsley (40 matches); **20** Jonny Wilkinson (28 victories).

QUIZ 4: ENGLAND AT THE RUGBY WORLD CUP

1 Australia, lost 19–6, 1987; **2** Japan, won 60–7, 1987; **3** Mike Harrison, v Japan; **4** 111–13 v Uruguay, 2003; **5** 0–36 v South Africa, 2007; **6** Australia and South Africa (5); **7** New Zealand (3 defeats); **8** Tonga (137 points in two matches); **9** Scotland (25 points in two matches); **10** Georgia (18 tries in two matches); **11** Jason Leonard (22 matches); **12** Jonny Wilkinson and Jason Leonard (18); **13** Rory Underwood (11 tries); **14** Jonny Wilkinson (277 points); **15** Jason Robinson (v Australia, 2003 final); **16** Josh Lewsey (5 v Uruguay, 2003); **17** Paul Grayson (36 v Tonga, 1999); **18** Joe Worsley (v Uruguay, 2003); **19** Rob Andrew (17 v Italy, 2005); **20** Will Carling and Martin Johnson (11).

QUIZ 5: ENGLAND CHAMPIONS OF THE WORLD
1 Neil Back; **2** Paul Grayson; **3** Ben Cohen and Will Greenwood; **4** Will Greenwood; **5** Neil Back, Phil Vickery and Iain Balshaw – the fourth try in that match was a penalty try; **6** Phil Vickery; **7** Nine – Stuart Abbott, Iain Balshaw (2), Mike Catt (2), Andy Gommarsall (2), Will Greenwood, Josh Lewsey (5), Dan Luger, Lewis Moody and Jason Robinson (2); **8** Will Greenwood; **9** Three; **10** Jason Robinson; **11** Dorian West, Martin Corry and Kyran Bracken; **12** Lawrence Dallaglio; **13** Josh Lewsey and Will Greenwood (five tries); **14** Jason Leonard and Lewis Moody (four); **15** Laurence Dallaglio, Martin Johnson, Jason Leonard, Lewis Moody, Jason Robinson and Phil Vickery; **16** Martin Corry and Danny Grewcock; **17** Dorian West (born: 5 Oct 1967); **18** Jonny Wilkinson (born: 25 May 1979); **19** Dan Luger (Perpignan); **20** Australia Prime Minister John Howard.

QUIZ 6: ENGLAND AT TWICKENHAM
1 Wales, won 11–3, 15 Jan 1910; **2** Scotland (38 wins in 47 matches); **3** New Zealand (16 defeats in 22 matches); **4** 134–0 v Romania, 17 Nov 2001; **5** 42–6 v South Africa, 22 Nov 2008; **6** Fred Chapman, v Wales, 15 Jan 1910; **7** Rory Underwood (27 tries); **8** Jonah Lomu (New Zealand – 5 tries); **9** Rory Underwood (5 v Fiji, 4 Nov 1989); **10** Jonny Wilkinson (650 points); **11** Dan Carter (New Zealand – 97 points); **12** Charlie Hodgson (44 points v Romania, 17 Nov 2001); **13** Christophe Lamaison (France – 28 points v New Zealand, RWC 1999); **14** Gethin Jenkins (Wales – 4 March 2000); **15** Jason Robinson (v Scotland, 22 March 2003); **16** Cyril Brownlie (New Zealand – 3 Jan 1925); **17** Lewis Moody (v Samoa, 26 Nov 2005); **18** Jason Leonard (55 appearances); **19** Colin Gibson (Ireland) and Fabien Pelous (France) – eight appearances; **20** Lewis Moody (13 defeats in 35 matches between 2001 and 2011).

QUIZ 7: ENGLAND RECORDS
1 Colin Laird (18 years 124 days); **2** Frederick Gilbert (38 years 362 days); **3** Jason Leonard (114 caps); **4** Peter Winterbottom (58 caps); **5** Simon Shaw (15 years between his first and last cap); **6** Will Carling (44 matches); **7** Jonny Wilkinson (1,179 points); **8** Charlie Hodgson (44 points v Romania, Twickenham, 17 Nov 2001); **9** Jon Webb (296 points); **10** Bill Beaumont (21 matches); **11** Rory Underwood (49 tries); **12** Daniel Lambert (v France, 1907), Rory Underwood (v Fiji, 1989) and Josh Lewsey (v Uruguay, 2003); **13** Mike Harrison (v Japan, 1987); **14** Josh Lewsey (v Uruguay, 2003) and Mark Cueto (v Romania, 2011); **15** Chris Ashton (six in 2011); **16** Cyril Lowe (eight in 1914); **17** 14 matches (March 2002–June 2003); **18** 2001; **19** Ten matches (1922–25); **20** Eight matches (2003–07).

QUIZ 8: ENGLAND CAPTAINS
1 Will Carling (59 matches); **2** Dave Davies; **3** Martin Weston (two wins in five matches, 1963–68); **4** Will Carling (49 points); **5** Will Carling (11 tries); **6** Will Carling and Chris Robshaw (14 defeats); **7** Norman Wodehouse in 1913; **8** Fred Stokes (1871), Frederick Alderson (1891), Joe Mycock (1947) and Nigel Melville (1984); **9** Rob Andrew (v Italy, Durban, 31 May 1995) and Jonny Wilkinson (v South Africa, Pretoria, 2 June 2007) – 17 points; **10** Ronald Poulton-Palmer (4 v France, Colombes, 13 Apr 1914); **11** France; **12** New Zealand; **13** Lennard Stokes (1880–81); **14** Bill Beaumont (1978–82); **15** Dickie Jeeps (4 draws in 13 matches, 1960–62); **16** Rob Andrew and Mike Tindall (both won their only match as England captain); **17** Mike Harrison (50 per cent); **18** Will Carling and Martin Johnson – 11; **19** Mike Harrison (20 points); **20** Martin Corry (33 years 351 days, England v South Africa at the Stade de France in the Rugby World Cup 2007 final).

QUIZ 9: ENGLAND AGAINST SOUTH AFRICA, NEW ZEALAND AND AUSTRALIA (SANZAR)
1 20 December 1969 (11–8 at Twickenham – in their sixth match against South Africa);
2 7 January 1928 (18–11 at Twickenham – in their second match against Australia);
3 On 4 January 1936 (13–0 at Twickenham – in their third match against New
Zealand); **4** 3 June 1972 (18–9 at Johannesburg – in their first-ever away match against
South Africa); **5** 21 June 2003 (25–14 at Melbourne – in their 11th away match against
Australia); **6** 15 September 1973 (16–10 at Auckland – in the second away match
against New Zealand); **7** Australia (18 wins); **8** New Zealand (seven wins); **9** 53–3 (at
Twickenham on 23 Nov 2002); **10** 10–58 (at Bloemfontein on 26 May 2007); **11** 20–3
(at Twickenham on 17 Nov 1973); **12** 0–76 (at Brisbane on 6 June 1998); **13** 38–21
(at Twickenham on 1 Dec 2012); **14** 22–64 (at Dunedin on 20 June 1998); **15** Jonny
Wilkinson (294 points); **16** Owen Farrell (107 points); **17** Ben Cohen (seven tries);
18 Rob Andrew (v South Africa, Pretoria, 4 June 1994), Jonny Wilkinson (v South
Africa, Bloemfontein, 24 June 2000) and Charlie Hodgson (v South Africa, Twickenham,
20 November 2004) – 27 points; **19** Alexander Obolensky (v NZ), Bob Lloyd (v NZ),
Rory Underwood (v Aus and v NZ), Will Carling (v NZ), Matt Perry (v Aus), Ben Cohen
(v Aus), Will Greenwood (v SA), Topsy Ojo (v NZ), Chris Ashton (v Aus), Ben Youngs
(v SA) and Ben Morgan (v Aus) – two tries; **20** Jason Leonard (28 matches).

QUIZ 10: ENGLAND AWAY
1 Ireland (32 wins); **2** Ireland (1–0, Dublin, 13 Dec 1875 – in England's fourth away
match); **3** New Zealand (at Auckland on 25 May 1963 – England lost 11–21; **4** Romania
and USA (1 win); **5** Wales (36); **6** France (673 points in 49 matches); **7** Ireland (106
tries in 66 matches); **8** 58–3 v Romania, Bucharest, 13 May 1989; **9** 0–76 v Australia,
Brisbane, 6 June 1998; **10** Jason Leonard (42 appearances); **11** Rory Underwood
(15 tries); **12** Jonny Wilkinson (326 points); **13** Paul Grayson (128), Dusty Hare (128),
Rob Andrew (126), Jonathan Webb (115) and Owen Farrell (113); **14** Dave Walder
(29 points v Canada, Burnaby Lake, 9 June 2001); **15** Arthur Hudson (v France, Paris,
22 Mar 1906), Ronald Poulton-Palmer (v France, Colombes, 13 Apr 1914) and Chris
Oti (v Romania, Bucharest, 13 May 1989) – 4; **16** Howard Marshall (v Wales, Cardiff, 7
Jan 1893); **17** 27 – 27–36 v South Africa, Johannesburg, 16 June 2012 and 27–28 v New
Zealand, Dunedin, 14 Jun 2014; **18** Will Carling (24 matches); **19** Mike Burton
(v Australia, Brisbane, 31 May 1975); **20** Danny Grewcock (v New Zealand, Dunedin,
20 Jun 1998) and Simon Shaw (v New Zealand, Auckland, 19 Jun 2004).